At Rainbow's End

A Journey of Spirit Discovery and Freedom From Addiction

By
Mary Christensen

PublishAmerica
Baltimore

© 2004 by Mary Christensen.
All rights reserved. No part of this book may be reproduced, stored in a retrieval system or transmitted in any form or by any means without the prior written permission of the publishers, except by a reviewer who may quote brief passages in a review to be printed in a newspaper, magazine or journal.

First printing

ISBN: 1-4137-1982-1
PUBLISHED BY PUBLISHAMERICA, LLLP
www.publishamerica.com
Baltimore

Printed in the United States of America

DEDICATION:

To all of you who suffer from addiction in all of its various disguises; that you too, may find freedom.

Acknowledgments

I would like to acknowledge my dear husband Lee for his love and support. I also want to thank him for the computer and teaching me how to use it. I couldn't have written this book without him.

I would like to acknowledge my children Michael and Kayla for being such a powerful presence of love and light in my life. They are beautiful beings and my world is a better place because of them.

I would like to acknowledge my parents, Betty and Fran Dale, for their loving guidance and support throughout my life. They have been my greatest teachers and I love them with all of my heart and soul.

I would like to acknowledge my dear sister Julie Dregne, for finding her own freedom and showing me it could be done. I appreciate all of her encouraging words and wisdom. I also want to acknowledge her for writing and recording her CD, "HAWK SHE SOARS." It has been a great source of inspiration and strength for me. I would also like to acknowldge her husband Tim Dregne and her daughter Sarah Sloniker for their love and support.

I want to acknowledge my brother David Dale for being a shining example of peace and love. I appreciate all of his love and support.

I would like to acknowledge my dear sister Kathi, her husband Don and their children Kelsey and Jared, for their love and support.

I want to acknowledge Sue Christensen for her love and support.

I want to acknowledge Virginia Durgin for her friendship, love and support.

I want to acknowledge Tammy Carmen for her friendship, love and support.

I want to acknowledge Gary and Barb Christensen for their love and support.

I want to thank the Foundation for Inner Peace for giving me permission to quote from A Course in Miracles.

I would like to acknowledge PublishAmerica for giving my book a chance and publishing it.

Last but not least, I want to thank God and the power of love to transform our lives.

I cannot find the words to fully express how deeply I feel about everyone I have known in my life. My sister Julie wrote a song that really comes close to expressing how I feel. The song is called "Touching my Soul" and I dedicate it to you.

"TOUCHING MY SOUL"

Thank you to all I have known in my life
For putting your footprints on my path
For coloring my canvas in so many different shades
And for touching my soul.

Did I work with you in a flower shop on the outskirts of town
Or in a bookstore that turned my life around
Were you a close friend whose path took a different turn than mine
Were you a teacher who encouraged me to learn?

Everyone you meet writes a page in the story of your life.
Some play main roles
Others just pass through
But large or small, good or bad
My life would not be the same
Without knowing you

Did I meet you in a coffee shop on a rainy afternoon?
Did we sing a song together years gone by

MARY CHRISTENSEN

Did we stand together in a check out line that took some time
Or did you simply smile and say hi?

To my husband, son and daughter
Mother and father
Sisters and brother
Close friends and family
Thank you
For filling my life with love

Thank you to all I have known in my life
For putting your footprints on my path
For coloring my canvas in so many different shades
And for
Touching my soul

By Julie Dregne

Introduction

The search for the pot of gold at the end of the rainbow is a journey that extends to the depths of eternity. The treasure cannot be found outside of our self and so the search through external sources is unlimited. Alcoholism, food addiction, and the endless list of addictions and disorders, are only the beginning of the relentless search for peace of mind and freedom where it cannot be found.

Peace of mind and freedom can also be sought through the fanatical pursuit of dreams. If only I am successful enough or rich enough or secure enough, I will have peace of mind and freedom. However, as many people can testify, freedom cannot be found there either. Another goal and then another becomes the means to which they can find their freedom. So where is freedom if it cannot be found in externals? And how do we free our minds from the trap of addiction?

Freedom is our original birthright. Contrary to popular belief, God created us perfect in his/her image. Why would creation create imperfection and then give their creation commands and orders to control it? As a child I often contemplated and challenged the ideas and beliefs of the church. Many of the ideas simply did not make sense to me and no one seemed to have the answers to the questions entertained in my mind. My father was the minister and even he did not have an answer that registered as a truth. A God "out there" who watched over everything we did and condemned us for our wrongdoings just didn't make sense. For instance, if we were given free will, then why all of the commandments? *"That is why the Holy Spirit never commands. To command is to assume inequality, which the Holy Spirit demonstrates, does not exist." (ACIM, I. p.103, 11; 1and 2).*

Now I understand the commandments are there because they are natural laws of cause and effect. They were instruments to teach people how to live according to the natural laws of God. When you know who you are, they are not even necessary. Violating these natural laws has a direct consequence to your own well being. I do not consider them orders directed by a fearful God who will punish us if they are violated.

I always knew God was about Love and not fear. Over the course of my life, I have tried many different churches and denominations. I have found that fear is the central theme surrounding most religions. I am not against religion. All roads lead to God. I simply disagree with using fear to teach about God. God and fear do not belong together in any form.

I have never been a person who believes something simply because someone tells me it is true. I have to find out for myself. "How does God know everything we're thinking and feeling?" "He just does." This wasn't good enough for me. I had to know for myself. The explanations closely resembled those of Santa Claus. How could he get around the world in one night delivering gifts to all the children of the world? Of course it turned out to be a tale, along with all of the other tales that are told to children for fun. So what was I to believe? Thus began the quest for truth and the search for freedom.

My quest for truth appeared to be through the back door. Nevertheless, I learned through all of my experiences as they taught me where not to find it. I began by looking for freedom in all of the wrong places. I started abusing alcohol at a very young age. Alcohol seemed to give me the peace and comfort I so desperately longed for in my life. The consequences of alcohol abuse were anything but pleasant and I always knew it was not the answer. I continued on and off with alcohol abuse for many years.

I wasn't aware that peace of mind could be achieved from within. Of course, at the time I wasn't even aware that I was searching for peace. Now I am aware of what it is I was attempting to teach myself throughout my life. There were no mistakes, just misadventures that ultimately revealed themselves. As with everything else in my life I was seeking to control my world externally to achieve peace.

I still sought God outside of myself. I wasn't even aware of what I was creating in my life until I opened my eyes to discovering myself through meditation and contemplation. A COURSE IN MIRACLES came across my path and has been a tremendous instrument in discovering the power of my own Spirit. It is the foundation for the inner peace I experience now.

So here I am, a thirty-eight-year-old wife and mother of two beautiful children. I have discovered the keys to freedom from addiction and I would like to share them with the world. I know I am not the first person to have an insight into peace and freedom but I would like to add my personal flavor to the teachings of A COURSE IN MIRACLES and how it has assisted me in finding freedom from addiction.

I realized freedom from addiction when I was able to make the connection in my mind between addiction and the thoughts and beliefs I held. I knew there was another way to live life. I simply had to know it was possible in order to achieve it. I had to desire freedom more than I wanted bondage to alcohol or anything else for that matter. I asked the Holy Spirit for help and my mind was freed. It was a gradual process that took dedication, persistence and enough relapses to know I didn't want to be a prisoner to alcohol any longer. I had to realize that I had control over the thoughts I allowed myself to think and that I wasn't powerless over anything unless I gave it power.

Eventually, I realized that I had to let go of every definition I had of myself in order to make room for truth. If I think I already know who I am, then it isn't likely I am going to discover anything new. Getting rid of the self that I had created was the first step in discovering my true identity. I had to be willing to let go of defining myself and allow my Spirit to reveal it to me.

From a young age we are programmed to believe whatever it is we are taught. The mind has the power to take any belief and make it a reality. If the belief stems from a feeling of lack and limitation, then our experience will reflect it. God created us perfect. If we choose to see ourselves as less than the divine and glorious beings that we are, then our lives will mirror this belief. Nevertheless, our true identity is always there ready and waiting to be discovered. Our divinity and freedom of expression is omnipresent.

We create everything in our lives. We are all children of God learning about how our thoughts, beliefs and feelings create our reality. Nevertheless, people continue on with their everyday lives, never questioning their own ideas and beliefs. Usually those beliefs are acquired through an authority figure they dare not question because they are certain to have all of the answers. If it is a Doctor or priest or someone they trust the person is more likely to commit to the belief. The beliefs can be destructive and cruel and all in the name of God. People suffer and die because they refuse to question their own beliefs.

How many times has a doctor told a patient they have only so much time left to live? If the person is convinced they are going to die in six months, there is not much chance of recovery. There are many cases of unexplained healings as well. Doctor's should not be allowed to give death sentences because there is never a way of knowing the outcome for certain; unless the patient is convinced they are going to die.

Oftentimes religious organizations convince the members they are shameful and need to regularly atone for their sins. The members must attend church regularly or they feel guilty. This is surely one way to guarantee the survival of a business. Rather than seeking to know God from within, they rely on Priests or other authority figures to guide their lives. There have even been crimes committed against children by some of the priests. They have covered it up for years and apparently they have no need to atone for their sins. Nevertheless, people continue to belong to the organization because their beliefs are firmly tied to it. I am sure many people still believe a priest would never do such a thing. This must be how they allow themselves to continue to be a part of something they know is wrong. After all, how can you take direction from someone who uses their position to take advantage of children?

Beliefs as well as thoughts can be changed. Beliefs are relative and can change with the thinker. A belief is not a knowing, for if you know something it simply is, and you don't have to put your faith in it. You only need faith in a belief, when you have doubt to begin with. If you know without a doubt that you are safe, is there any point in believing in protection?

Thoughts are not something that happen to us. We are the thinkers of the thoughts and not the thoughts themselves. One day while I was out for a walk I noticed I was focusing on what was not there in my life. I was feeling rather anxious and afraid. I remember acknowledging the fear that encompassed my mind. It suddenly occurred to me that I did not have to change anything but what I was thinking. Sure enough, my world changed instantly. It no longer seemed to cave in around me. I experienced the changes automatically as I switched my focus to everything I was grateful for in my life. I no longer felt powerless. I had the power to feel good about my life.

We have the power to create our life any way we would like it to be. If we have created lack, limitation, pain and sorrow, we have the same power to change it around. We create our own reality. That is the good news. We can put faith in the world and what other people say is truth or we can look within and let the truth be revealed. The world does not happen to us. It is in place as a reflection of you. According to *A COURSE IN MIRACLES,* there is no world. *"There is no world apart from what you wish, and herein lies your ultimate release. Change but your mind on what you want to see, and all the world must change accordingly." (ACIM, II. p.242, 5; 1and2)* Freedom is the result of this realization.

We can experience anything we want to in this life. We can create whatever it is our hearts desire. It is all there for the asking. The greatest freedom comes from realizing that nothing happens to us without our permission. We can continue to create from fear and limitation or we can create through love and knowingness.

Discovering our Spirit is a fundamental key to finding freedom from addiction. When we are blind to our divinity we believe the world is something that happens to us. We tend to blame other people or situations for the happenings in our own minds. We need to continuously rearrange the external world to change how we feel inside. True freedom comes from knowing we have the power to change our own life and experience whatever it is we choose to experience. We are not victims of the world. We are the creators of the world we choose to see.

Addiction

Addiction is the result of a mind seeking to control the body's feelings through external means. The body is the central focus of an addictive personality. To change how a person feels, the body needs to be altered chemically. This is one of the core beliefs of an addict. Do you realize you can change how you feel by changing your mind? It is that simple. There is nothing outside of you that can do this for you and last. There are not enough stars in the sky for all of the substances you will need to change your feelings externally. You will never get enough of a substance because you are looking in the wrong place. You can change your thoughts here and now. You are a direct result of whatever you are thinking in this moment. If you want to change how you are feeling, then change your thoughts.

Change takes place in your mind. If you feel controlled by an addictive behavior, you cannot change your behavior by just changing what you do because you will feel at the mercy of the behavior. As an alcoholic, you can quit drinking for a while. You will change your behavior temporarily but eventually you will find yourself going down the same line at the liquor store. If you try to change your behavior you will be changing the symptom and not the problem. The problem is your mind and this is where you need to create change. You will soon realize that it is as simple to change your mind, as it is to feel at the mercy of it. *"I have said that you cannot change your mind by changing your behavior, but I have also said, and many times, that you can change your mind. When your mood tells you that you have chosen wrongly, and this is so whenever you are not joyous, then know this need not be."(ACIM, I. p.63, 2; 1, 2.)*

Where do you begin to release your mind from the trap of addiction?

First you have to realize you are not powerless and at the mercy of your own thoughts. You do have the power to change them and make good decisions for your life. As an alcoholic or addict you have to feel pretty powerless in your life. Drinking alcohol to feel good is only temporary and the consequences are horrendous. Why would a person put poison in their mouth so they can feel high? I know that if you overindulge for enjoyment you certainly do not feel joy to begin with and therefore need to falsely create it.

To feel true joy and peace within is a part of discovering who you are. You are not at the mercy of your thoughts and feelings; you are the creator of them. To awaken from the dream is to awaken to the acknowledgment of your divinity. When you deny yourself the power to create good feelings in your life, you seek out substances that will do it for you. That is really the bottom line.

It won't take years of therapy to be free. It can happen in an instant. You just have to be willing to free your mind from the traps you have created. *"An "imprisoned" mind is not free because it is possessed, or held back, by itself. It is therefore limited, and the will is not free to assert itself." (ACIM, I. p.39, 4; 3,4)* You don't necessarily need to know how to go about achieving freedom. You just need to be willing to unlearn everything you think you know now. Your mind just needs a willing participant in order for you to be released from your own self-inflicted limitations.

Food

The significant problems with weight in this country are a prime example of how our thoughts create. It is obvious dieting doesn't work. The law is what you resist will persist. The more energy you put out trying to suppress your appetite, the greater it gets. If you focus on food, then that is all you will think about. The moment you tell yourself you need to lose weight, where is your attention? Most likely it is on food.

If you need to lose weight, simply make the decision to do it. You have to know it is possible. If you can't see it in your mind, it is not going to happen. Focus on what it feels like to be slender, light and energetic. Send loving thoughts to your body. Retraining your mind will take dedication and persistence. Recognize it is not your body you dislike. It is the negative thoughts you have towards your body that need to change.

Weight loss is not about food. It is about changing your mind about you. It is important to realize that you have created your body with negative thoughts and feelings and you are free to change it as well. I often hear people saying, "I can gain weight just from looking at food." The messages you tell yourself about food determine how you experience it. Food doesn't make you fat. The thoughts you tell yourself that lead to overindulgence are what creates weight gain. If you try to control how you feel inside through food, you will overindulge because you will never get enough. You will always need more to feel good. Careful monitoring of the thoughts you allow yourself to think is the most important step you can take in loving and caring for your body. There are some people that can eat whatever they want and never gain weight. If you would like to have the same experience it would be a good idea to explore the thoughts and feelings they hold about food.

When you eat, enjoy your food. Be fully present when you are eating. Don't be thinking about your dessert while you're eating your main course. If you are reading or watching TV while you are eating, you are not taking the time to enjoy your food. Be fully present when you are eating and you won't need to eat as much to feel satisfied. If you overeat, never hate your body for it. It only responds to what your mind tells it to do.

Be thankful for the food you are eating. Many people starve to death and would give anything to trade places with you. Most importantly, ask your Spirit for guidance. Your Spirit will assist you in changing your mind about you. You can refer to your Spirit in any manner you choose. Use whatever words you must, whether it be your higher self or higher power or any other words. Do not get hung up on words because they cannot possibly define God anyway.

When you make the shift to an internal focus, you will not see food as a source of fulfillment. The urge to overeat will leave you and you will tend to choose healthier foods. It is your thinking you need to change. You have the power to create good feelings in your life without using food. If you simply try to control what you are eating you are working on the symptom and not the problem.

If you simply cannot lose weight, you most likely have an underlying fear. There is always an accompanying belief. If you monitor your conscious thoughts, you will discover what is in your unconscious. Many people feel they are victims of their unconscious. This is not true unless you make it true. If you want to know what is in your unconscious mind, explore the beliefs and thoughts you hold in your conscious mind. Your conscious mind is the programmer of the unconscious.

Extra weight must serve a purpose for you or you wouldn't allow it. It is often a form of protection. Again, monitor your thoughts and you will discover what purpose it serves for you. The truth is within you and you have the power to discover it. It is there for the asking. I do not have a doctor's degree so I may not be authorized to give such advice. Take what rings as truth for you and discard the rest. You are your own authority.

It is important to take good care of yourself but if you place value on your appearance above all else, then you have become addicted to the way you look. Somehow you have come to believe that it is your appearance that gives you value. The simple fact that you exist is enough to make you valuable.

We are all equal in the eyes of God. Our true essence cannot be seen with the naked eye and it is here that our value lies. If we spend all of our time placing value on our appearance, we are living an illusion and have misplaced our identity. I have heard extremely beautiful women comment that they were not happy about the way they looked. I am talking about celebrities who must believe their careers are based upon their looks. If beauty is where salvation is, then plastic surgery ought to do the trick. Addiction has many forms and as long as feelings or states of being are connected with a source outside of our self, there will be an addiction.

There was a time in my life when my identity was tied up in being slender. I was never happy about the way I looked. There was always something else about my appearance that needed to change. If you think your power in life belongs to your appearance, then you will be frantically searching for ways to improve it. It will never be good enough because you will be looking in the wrong place. You can change how you feel about yourself with your thoughts; the God given power of creation. Choose to feel good about who you really are and be willing to discover it.

Addiction to food also takes the form of anorexia when the person believes their value lies in controlling the amount they do not eat. Somehow they come to believe that starvation is appealing and the skinnier they are, the more beautiful they become. The problem with this belief is they are never slender enough. Some people literally starve themselves to death. They are striving to feel good about themselves by altering their body. If you do not love yourself, changing your body will not do it for you.

The media has convinced many of you that skin and bones are appealing. Of course the media also uses starving children to appeal to the hearts of those for money to help the poor. The mind is powerful and a person can convince their mind this is appealing. The problem lies in thinking your value is determined by your appearance. True beauty comes from within. You can learn to love yourself when you stop identifying yourself as your body.

When you identify yourself as your body, your primary focus is on controlling how it looks and feels. You forget about your true essence and the power of your own Spirit. You separate yourself from God and one another. You strive to achieve freedom and peace of mind by changing your body. This is not the way to find freedom. I can assure you that true freedom and peace of mind are not about the body at all. When you discover them as a part of who you are, your body will function perfectly as well.

Alcoholism

I am an expert in alcoholism. I have 25 years of experience either drinking or quitting drinking. I have learned a great deal through my experiences. Alcoholism is merely the search for peace and happiness in an outside substance. Until the connection is made between the thought and the substance, use and abuse will continue.

Freedom from alcoholism is possible as with any disorder or disease. It is not as difficult as it is considered to be. Alcoholism is not a label you need to carry around with you for the rest of your life. Freedom does not consist of bondage in any form. When you are free from substance abuse, you no longer desire it or think about it because you know that you simply change your mind. "*Your ability to direct your thinking as you choose is part of its power. If you do not believe you can do this you have denied the power of your thought, and thus rendered it powerless in your belief.*" (ACIM, I.p.123, 2; 6 and 7)

You are not powerless. "*Faith given to illusions does not lack power, for by it does the Son of God believe he is powerless.*" (ACIM, I. P. 452; 5, 3) If you believe you are powerless, your faith will be rewarded. You always have the power to choose what you think and experience in life. Addiction can be a powerful tool to discover the power of your own mind. You must simply be willing to release your mind from the traps you have created.

People that quit drinking often replace the addiction with some other repetitive behavior. Their thoughts of well-being are linked with a substance. Those same thoughts and feelings can be experienced without the substance. Euphoria can be achieved through the awareness of your divinity and the power of your own creative potential.

I used to think that feelings happened to me. When I didn't like the bad feelings I was having, then I would drink. Alcohol seemed to make me feel better. When I discovered it was as simple as changing my mind, then alcohol was no longer needed. The substance was never the cure. I believed alcohol made me feel better. In reality, I was changing my mind all along. The alcohol was only the link.

Anytime, you have a behavior you do not like and feel you cannot control, close your eyes and capture the feelings you get from it. The good feelings are not outside of you and never have been. Take shopping for instance. People become shop-a-holics because of the good feelings they get when purchasing something new. They struggle because they end up with all this stuff they do not want and expenses they do not need. I was never a shop-a-holic but one day I found myself wanting to go shopping for no valid reason at all. It was then I made the connection that it was the feelings I desired. I envisioned the feelings within myself and I no longer felt the urge to go shopping.

We do things for the feelings we think we get from them. Whenever we continuously repeat a behavior or take a substance for the satisfaction it brings us, then rest assured peace will not be a result. We will always need that substance or activity to bring us peace. Addiction can take many forms but there is only one answer, and it is found within.

Pursuing dreams in an effort to feel self worth is also a form of addiction. If a person reaches a certain level of worldly success in disregard of his or her Spirit, then the pursuit will be relentless and satisfaction will never be attained. If something should happen to the accumulated wealth, status or worldly "power", the person is devastated because it was their personal foundation.

When a person seeks truth and the proper alignment of Spirit with their personal life, there is nothing that can destroy their foundation. For it is based on truth and not illusion. No longer are you struggling to validate your self worth. You create simply for the sake of creating and expressing your being. You no longer seek the approval or validation of others, for you know you are already everything. You are more than any definition the world has for you. I AM.

I AM, is a powerful statement of truth. When you come to understand the power of "I AM," you stop defining yourself, for any definition is a limitation. You are whatever you choose to think, feel and believe. Every moment you choose your thoughts. You will learn to experience freedom when you recognize that you hold the keys to your own salvation. If you wait around for someone else to do it, you will be waiting a long time.

Control

Let's discuss the problems associated with the need to control. Control is a form of self-punishment that lasts indefinitely in a mind searching for freedom through external manipulation. Why self-punishment? Control perpetuates itself in a cyclical, rather insane fashion. Control is never really accomplished; it merely holds the illusion that it succeeds. The person frantically searches for a means to accomplish a hold of sorts, on people, situations, or things, that seem to have significance to a state of mind they declare as valuable. In reality, it is a personal hell the person has created in their mind.

When we succumb to the knowledge of who we are, control becomes valueless. When we recognize we are love, do we need to strive to achieve it? A state of mind viewed from a whole perspective, doesn't need to change events or people to achieve peace. It is an omnipresent state of being where peace is inherently present.

A person stuck in the realm of control may not recognize the cause of their behavior. It may not seem sane to them, but nevertheless the behavior continues. If the behavior is never questioned, the person will not be free from it. Chances are the person continues to place blame on someone else for the insanity of their own actions. In this case, the person cannot be free. We can only change ourselves. If we live our lives by failing to take responsibility for our own thoughts, beliefs and attitudes, then we become a victim of ourselves. We are victimized by our own mind.

To achieve freedom from the need to control, you must relinquish your thoughts and definitions of safety. You may feel safe as long as you are in control, and foolishly afraid when you feel out of control. The safety you experience is in direct proportion to the notions you have about it. If you feel a sense of safety when your house is cluttered full of junk and you can hardly walk in it, then you will frantically collect junk. Your mind will be relentlessly trapped into needing junk. If a burglar cannot even get into your house then certainly he will leave you alone. Your belief in it can be so strong you have to do whatever it takes to feel safe. Of course the opposite is true for some people; you do not feel safe or comfortable around clutter. If this is true to an extreme, you often feel out of control whenever the environment is not in perfect order according to your expectations. A true sense of safety comes from within. It is not acquired by outside means but is merely recognized. When we come to recognize the power inherent within ourselves, we know it as our source of safety.

A person may be obsessed with seeking the love of another through attempting to gain a false sense of power and control over them. They blindly think the person needs to be manipulated in order to keep them in a relationship with them. The opposite is actually true. Controlling someone eventually pushes them away. Love is not something to achieve through manipulation or control. It is a state of being that is shared with another person. If a person is living in the world of illusion, they will think love is something to attain outside of them. Their search will be relentless and freedom will not be found.

"Our sense of inadequacy, weakness and incompletion comes from the strong investment in the 'scarcity principle' that governs the whole world of illusions. From that point of view, we seek in others what we feel is wanting in ourselves. We 'love' another in order to get something ourselves. That, in fact, is what passes for love in the dream world. There can be no greater mistake than that, for love is incapable of asking for anything. (ACIMp.xi preface)

Control is a form of addiction. The cause is always the same. A person is simply trying to change the way they feel inside, through external manipulation. If something can be taken from you, it is not a real sense of safety or security. When you know safety and security within, you will always feel safe and secure and nothing can take it away from you.

Control is the central focus of a person experiencing life through the eyes of separation. The connection we share is ignored and life is a struggle. It is a struggle because we are constantly fighting against the natural flow of life. It is like fish swimming upstream. When we put our attention inward and quiet our minds, we will find peace has always been with us. Peace is our natural state of being. Whenever we begin to try to control events externally, it only leads to irritation, frustration and anger. If we align our mind with peace, we feel release from fear and we can create from a space of knowingness and trust.

Sometimes it is hard to believe you are not at the mercy of your own thoughts. At times you may even feel completely out of control. Whenever this is true, your ego is in charge of the show. You have allowed separation and fear to determine the course of your thoughts and feelings. At any moment you have the choice to choose peace rather than fear. You can be amidst intense fear and suddenly choose to let it go, allowing peace to overflow your being. It can happen in an instant, as soon as you change your mind.

Fear

You can choose thoughts of fear or love. Fear is an illusion and love is a reflection of truth. Fear is a result of identifying with the ego or limited self. It is illusory because it is not what God intended for you to experience. The ego merely dreams a dream, which it thinks is real. The foundation of the ego is weak because it does not really exist. Only truth is real and remains regardless of whether or not it is acknowledged. You can alter your perception of truth but you cannot destroy it.

The presence of fear is a sure sign that the ego is in control because that is its purpose. Fear is disguised in anger, worry, anxiety, hatred, condemnation, and any emotion other than peace. Anger is an attack thought and is based on an incorrect perception. Truth never attacks, because only wholeness exists and would be perceived as an attack against itself. *"What you project you disown, and therefore do not believe is yours. You are excluding yourself by the very judgment that you are different from the one on whom you project. Since you have also judged against what you project, you continue to attack it because you continue to keep it separated. By doing this unconsciously, you try to keep the fact that you attacked yourself out of awareness, and thus imagine that you have made yourself safe." (ACIM, I. p.96, 2; 1-4)* You think you are protecting yourself from attack when you project it onto others.

Whenever you find yourself feeling angry, stop and ask yourself what is this really about? I can only be angry with someone if I think they hurt me in some way. No one actually has the power to hurt my feelings without my permission. My feelings are mine. They cannot be physically touched. Anger is only a mask. It is caused from feelings of pain or fear, which can only be present from the standpoint of the ego.

The ego needs validation of its feelings in order to feel self worth. It needs approval from "out there" to feel good. In reality, you are already everything and your Spirit doesn't require any validation. The ego is vigilant in approval seeking methods. Oftentimes it takes place without your conscious awareness, simply because you fail to recognize it.

Worry is the mental pursuit of potentially threatening outcomes that do not yet exist. Worry always stems from a fear of the past or future. Fear does not exist in the present moment. Worry is a waste of energy and many people are fatigued and depleted from this practice alone.

Anxiety would not be so prevalent if people let go of the idea of past and future. When a person learns to be fully present, anxiety will be non-existent. Anxiety is never based on a logical thought. It is only based on what-ifs and fears that are connected with a situation or place. Again, the focus of control is external and the person fails to realize it is not events that need controlling; they simply need to change their minds about them. I used to think that fear was something that happened to me. I now know I am in charge of what I think. Whenever I experience an emotion that brings emotional upheaval, I know it is a result of my thinking.

Jesus said there is nothing to fear but fear itself. I tend to agree with him. He was a man of great faith. His faith moved mountains and you could do the same. I think back to all the times I felt fear, and I know it did not produce any positive results. Whenever I had faith I know the outcome was nothing short of miraculous.

The existence of the ego depends on fear. You can learn to depend on your Spirit and trust in the perfect outcome in every circumstance. You choose between your Spirit and your ego to guide you at any given moment. Most assuredly the ego will lead you astray, creating problems and difficulties that could be avoided.

A lot of fear is simply learned. I remember when I was in about fourth grade and I rode my bike just about everywhere. I was at a friend's home and it had gotten dark outside before I left for home. Before I got on my bike to go home, a little girl asked me if I was afraid. Of course I had never even thought of being afraid until that moment. I remember the ride home that night quite clearly because fear pervaded my mind.

Some religions are based on fear. The central belief is that "we will help you avoid going to hell but you must follow this set of rules." In actuality, if you are fearful then you are already in hell. *"The Holy Spirit teaches thus: There is no hell. Hell is only what the ego has made of the present." (ACIM, I. P.302, 7; 1).*

When I was a young child I remember deciding to read the bible. I read it for a while before saying, "That is not the God I know and love." I knew that God would never spread fear and judgment. Some of the stories in the Bible are so violent. However there are certainly many good lessons to learn through the Bible. The problems become apparent when people interpret the messages from the standpoint of fear. *"These are some examples of upside-down thinking in the New Testament, although its gospel is really only the message of love. If the Apostles had not felt guilty, they never could have quoted me as saying, "I come not to bring peace but a sword." This is clearly the opposite of everything I taught." (ACIM, I. p.95, 15; 1-3)*

Many people fear the judgment of God after death. It is Man who judges. God is love and is not a source to be feared. Here and now is where we need to look at our own judgments of others and ourselves. When we judge another it is coming from ourselves and is but a reflection of you. There is no "other". We are one. When we release others, we are releasing ourselves as well. When we free our own mind, it includes everyone around us.

Fear is a word that is often associated with a devil. The devil is made real by their faith. There is one force. The ego and the devil can be put in the same category because neither of them really exists. Fear will manifest itself in whatever form the belief dictates. Do you have faith in God or the devil, love or fear?

It is not a good idea to follow someone who leads through fear. The best person to follow is the still small voice in your own mind. Listen to your own feelings and become accustomed to paying attention to them rather than disregarding them. When you do something and you feel it isn't right, there is often an unfavorable outcome that could have been avoided.

You can be free of problems because you are the creator of them. Do problems really exist, or is it your perception of events that create them in the first place? If your reality is created through your mind, then to rid yourself of problems, maybe you just need to stop believing in them. Perhaps you need to change the way you view the problems that are presently in your life so you can release them? What is there to change, except your mind?

I know I have experienced both heaven and hell in my own mind. It is a choice I make each moment. God did not create all the hatred and fear that is present on earth. It is not a part of God's plan for us. No, we cannot blame God for the bad things that happen to us. We need only look to ourselves. We are not separate from God and we never have been. The power we have to create simply manifests itself through the beliefs we hold about ourselves. If we believe we are alone and separate from God, then that will be our experience. When we come to realize our wholeness, it is simply an awakening to a state of being that we already are and always have been.

You cannot be in the present moment without faith. The present moment is where eternity is, and it is omnipresent. Fear and hell are really synonymous. Fear is simply not available in the present. Any time you experience it, you are in the past or future in your present state of mind. In other words you are not really thinking at all. You are dreaming a dream. If the dream has fear as a part of it, you could call it hell.

Imagine the detail involved in the making of a spider web. If one of God's creations can create this perfection, then God created us perfect too. Life is an intricately woven masterpiece when seen through the "eyes of wholeness".

Separation Verses Wholeness

I saw a road sign today that said to fear God and let go of evil. There is no way that love and fear can exist in the same category. It is ourselves we fear. Fear and evil are one, and only exist in a mind which perceives itself as separate from God. Separate minds and separate bodies are the central focus of this world. It is a world that is not real because it fails to recognize wholeness. People project, react and judge those they think they see outside of themselves rather than seeing the connection of our minds in the interaction of this reality. It is themselves they are truly attacking, judging and perceiving in forms they think are real. From the standpoint of wholeness, there is no one "out there" to attack. Separate bodies exist, but our minds are one. We are individual droplets of water in the body of the ocean. Our bodies may seem separate but our essence is shared.

The only "reality" is the one you think is real. You can get many people to agree with it, but nevertheless it was created by your mind and given the function you have decided for it. To align your perception with the Holy Spirit is to perceive truth. Only wholeness exists and the illusion of separation is what has created a world of fear. I suggest you take a good look in the mirror the next time you experience anger, pain, or suffering. It is you who have created these emotions through the process of separation. In order to relinquish fear and all of its corresponding emotions you simply choose peace. You choose the thoughts you think and any thought that is fear related needs to be cast away and replaced with peace. You have to begin by ridding yourself of everything in the way of knowing peace. Peace is available to you in an instant because it is a part of who you are. If you do not know how to do this, begin with the intention and invite the Holy Spirit to restore your mind to sanity.

Surrender to the recognition of your whole self; the one whom God created. We fight to maintain our separate identities as if there is a grand prize for such a venture. Feeling the need to maintain a separate identity simply encourages fear and its corresponding emotions. We compete with other people believing that superiority somehow exists. When we stop projecting fear onto others, we stop feeling it within. The world the ego created can indeed be surrendered when wholeness is recognized. Peace is automatically experienced in a mind transformed to see through the eyes of wholeness. *"Heaven is neither a place nor a condition. It is merely an awareness of perfect oneness, and the knowledge that there is nothing outside this oneness, and nothing else within." (ACIM P. 384, I. 1; 5 and 6)*

How we choose to define our lives is what determines our experiences. We have what we consider to be separate bodies having a separate experience. Our personalities or masks of our true identity, determine the part we play. We cavort about, unknowingly aware of our unity. Our bodies keep the illusion alive as long as we are focused on them. Our bodies are the central focus of the dream. We struggle to achieve a feeling of love and acceptance based upon what the body looks like or does. Of course, we consider ourselves to have low self-esteem if they do not live up to our expectations. They rarely do, because the very idea of focusing our attention on our bodies for fulfillment creates a constant battle of future-oriented states of being. In other words, I will be happy when or if I can get my body to look a certain way or accomplish a goal. If or when expectations are achieved, new ones are developed.

Health and or illness are also products of focused attention on the body. If you are in a perfect state of health, where is your attention? I can assure you it would not be on the body. If you have a headache and later on you notice it is gone, where is your attention? All of a sudden you have awareness that you do not have the pain anymore.

When the body is no longer considered a means for separation or attack, it will certainly be returned to its perfect state. It is the ego's use of the body that creates the physical problems we encounter. We compete against one another in ways that begin with thoughts of, "I am less than and need to prove I am greater." When we compete against someone with regards to anything, we are attempting to prove to ourselves that we can do or be better then someone else. The core belief is one of separation or there would not be any need to compete. Of course we can compete as a means to better ourselves but wholeness is already greater than anything it can ever prove.

There are numerous misuses of the body that come from the belief in separation. The ego perceives the body as the means to achieve freedom and salvation. Freedom of the mind and body are not achieved simultaneously. *"Minds are joined; bodies are not. Only by assigning to the mind the properties of the body does separation seem to be possible. And it is mind that seems to be fragmented and private and alone. Its guilt, which keeps it separate, is projected to the body, which suffers and dies because it is attacked to hold the separation in the mind, and let it not know its Identity." (ACIM, I. p.385, 3; 1-4)*

Our minds are one. We find we are much more than we once believed as we remove our attention from our bodies and allow our minds to reveal their true identity. It is the identification with our bodies that keeps us from reaching our truest potentials. Being without the body doesn't mean death but resurrection from existing ideas and beliefs about our self. Our minds are without limits; it is our bodies that experience limitation because of the properties we have assigned to them.

Freedom is achieved as wholeness is acknowledged. Addiction in any form is caused from identifying self with the body. A person struggles to find fulfillment through an act of changing how the body feels. Since the person thinks they are their body, they believe it is controlling their thoughts and feelings rather than their mind. In order to achieve freedom from the perceived restrictions of the body, they alter it chemically to change the way they feel.

Our bodies follow the commands of our minds. God did not create us in an inescapable prison called our bodies. We began identifying with our bodies and we created the illusion ourselves. *"If the mind can heal the body, but the body cannot heal the mind,"* then the mind must be stronger than the body." *(ACIM, I. p.105, 2; 6)* It is possible to be free from the constraints we have created in our lives. We have to be willing to allow the truth to be revealed to us. We simply have to be willing to see things differently and challenge our current beliefs that uphold our illusions. Put it this way; is the world of illusions worth upholding? Is your life working perfectly the way you have created it? Is there even a minute chance your life could be greatly improved? I know life is incredible and I am rediscovering it every day. I remember the life I used to live and I am now letting go of illusions, one by one.

A COURSE IN MIRACLES has been a wonderful instrument in teaching me to let go of everything that stands in the way of knowing inner peace. I recommend it to anyone who is willing to put forth the effort. I have been studying it for years and I tell you, it is a masterpiece that requires careful attention and worth every bit of effort. Many times it has validated my personal experiences. It is a light on the passageway to freedom and inner peace.

Forgiveness

Peace and Joy encompass the forgiving mind. When you no longer condemn or attack others with your thoughts, you free yourself. The moment you judge and attack another person with your thoughts, you experience the direct effects of those thoughts. You are not separate from the thoughts you think. When you project anger and hatred onto another person, you experience it yourself. Say you have an acquaintance and you don't particularly care for her because you have judged her reality. Where is the judgment coming from and whom does it really reflect? When you forgive others for their illusions, you are able to forgive yourself as well.

The presence of anger is a sure sign you are harboring attack thoughts. You don't need anger management courses to be released from anger. All you need to do is change your thoughts and the way you are viewing the situation or person. Simplicity is the name of the game. If you are around a person who is angry a lot of the time, it is best if you do not recognize it by connecting with it and sharing it. Oftentimes, when someone attacks you with anger, you attack back. When someone is angry, you feel his or her anger. If you simply react to someone's anger, it becomes yours as well. We are all connected and we experience the emotions and feelings of others. The key is letting go of the emotions and feelings you do not wish to experience. We do not have to be a victim of other people's emotions.

You actually change the way people respond to you when you change how you feel toward them. When it comes to relationships, it is always about you. You teach people how to respond to you. The way you feel about yourself is the key. You need to identify with the love that you are, rather than trying to get the love from someone else. The ego is needy and will need to control in order to feel loved. Relationships often fail because expectations can never be completely met. If he does not buy flowers for me on Valentines Day he does not love me. The list is endless.

If you spend your time judging the reality of others you have separated your mind from theirs and inevitably, conflict results. Then you have chosen chaos over peace, ego over Spirit. If you practice allowing rather than controlling or changing other people, you will find peace. It is through your desire to change other people or situations that ultimately leads to distress, resulting in unhappiness. Whatever you choose to think about other people, are the same guidelines with which you unknowingly judge yourself.

I remember a time when I used to get upset while driving in heavy traffic. If I got caught behind a driver that I thought didn't know how to drive a car, I would shout obscenities at them. I would allow anger to fill my mind and bring myself out of my calm peaceful center because I was reacting to them. One day, I realized it was more important for me to be at peace than it was for me to get filled with anger. I cannot separate myself from my projections. In other words,

I cannot be angry with someone without feeling the anger within my own being. Now I do not allow traffic problems to determine how I feel. Instead of getting all upset and full of fear in heavy traffic, I simply let it go. And do you know what? I rarely have any trouble while I am driving.

When you recognize yourself as the source of love, there is no need associated with it. The relationship is seen as an extension of yourself. You share yourself without expectations placed on the other person. I am love; perfect, whole and complete. I love to share the love that I am with you. If you project your love onto another, then you are separating yourself from love. Conditions are then placed on the love you expect to get in return.

From an ego state, love is defined in terms of what it can get from another person. I will give to you but I had better get something in return. When love is shared through the Holy Spirit, there are no conditions. It is a state of being that you share. Thus ends the struggle with yourself, and your relationships. As with addiction, the changes that need to take place are not outside of you.

Forgiveness is the window to the true reflection of the soul. When you forgive everyone you meet, you have forgiven yourself as well. You will see the Christ in everyone rather than a representation you have created through fear. It is almost as if the veil has been lifted and you discover spiritual insight includes everyone. *"Forgiveness is the healing of the perception of separation."(ACIM, I. p.46, 9;1)*.

True forgiveness doesn't really exist, because it is only for those who perceive separate minds. Our separate bodies simply mask the unity of our minds. The interplay regarding the perfect orchestration of life could not occur unless this was true. To truly forgive is to realize it isn't even necessary. Recognize you have created the situation and you can let it go and choose freedom instead.

It is your own feelings of guilt in life that chain you to your past. You are not able to forgive others or yourself unless you can let go of the guilt that torments your mind. *"If you allow yourself to feel guilty, you will reinforce the error rather than allow it to be undone for you." (ACIM, I. P.90, 5;5)* You cannot be free from habits or destructive addictions or behaviors as long as you continue to condemn yourself for them. If you do this, you put your attention on these behaviors and they repeat themselves.

In order to begin releasing your mind from guilt there are a few ideas you need to bring to the forefront of your mind. First of all, have the notion that you can be free of it. Introduce the idea of completely forgiving yourself for all of your perceived shortcomings or wrongdoings. Guilty feelings simply perpetuate negative feelings and the key to releasing yourself from the chains of your past is forgiveness. Of course, once you completely forgive yourself, you will find you no longer project condemnation or attack onto others. At the same time you are releasing yourself from the need to forgive others. What is there to forgive when everyone is already forgiven? *"When you feel guilty, remember that the ego has indeed violated the laws of God, but you have not. Leave the "sins" of the ego to me. That is what Atonement is for. But until you change your mind about those whom your ego has hurt, the Atonement cannot release you. While you feel guilty your ego is in command, because only the ego can experience guilt. This need not be."(ACIM, I. p.63, 5;1-6)*

It is a relief to know that it is your ego that creates guilt. Then you can be certain it is possible to be free from the constraints of guilt. I remember a time where I would allow someone else to make me feel guilty. I would reply, "You are just trying to make me feel guilty." Talk about being a victim here. No one can make you feel guilty including the ego. It can only create the perception that it is.

Many people may hold the belief that guilt is vital to the natural flow of life. If we don't feel guilty then we are horrible people. Then we have no conscience and can run around and do whatever we please. The very notion that guilt somehow makes you a better person is disturbing. Guilt and punishment are synonymous. One cannot exist without the other one. In order to feel guilty you have to feel you deserve punishment for your mistakes. The belief must presume that if you have enough sense to feel guilt, maybe you will correct your mistakes. You actually create the opposite effect when guilt is used to free you from your mistakes. It creates an illusion to support the behavior rather than release you from it.

This world is filled with criminals that have been convinced they have no chance of recovery. That is the only sin committed here. As a society we believe that crimes require punishment rather than correction and it costs us a great deal to maintain this belief. The belief in punishment just perpetuates the whole system. Our prisons are filled with people who feel helpless and powerless to change their life. They have been convinced by our society that they are wretched and sinful and can never change. Needless to say, we have a problem with overcrowding in prisons and those who are released, return to commit the crimes again.

If a person feels remorseful, they are given a lesser sentence. If they display no apparent guilt for their crimes, they are punished more severely. We are fearful of people who seem to carry no remorse or guilt. Surely they will commit their crime again. How do we know if someone really feels remorse when this can easily be staged anyway? I am not saying it is okay to commit horrific crimes. I am merely saying our society would greatly benefit by switching the focus to correction rather than punishment. It is called the department of corrections but the focus is on punishment.

Maybe it is because no one believes it is possible for a criminal to overcome his or her behavior. Like an alcoholic, they are forever at the mercy of uncontrolled thoughts and behaviors. This belief stems from the victim mentality this world encourages. The world operates under the system that perpetuates the very deeds it is attempting to eliminate.

I was watching a talk show one day and a man was explaining what he did to eliminate his behavior as a pedophile. Even though this man accomplished a victory he was still shunned by other people. Can you imagine having a problem that society labels as incurable? Then when you succeed at controlling your behavior, people still label you and "throw stones". This man was teaching other pedophiles to get support to overcome their behavior as well. This man obviously felt horribly about himself or he wouldn't have been able to commit such acts against children. Are we not encouraging him to feel bad about himself if we stay disgusted with him even after having the courage to seek help?

"If there is anyone among you that has not sinned, cast the first stone." Those may not be his exact words but wasn't Jesus trying to teach us something? We continue to worship him but we forget to live by his teachings. I had a dream one night about a pedophile. In the dream I heard his thoughts and I understood how badly he felt about committing these crimes against children, yet he felt helpless to change. The dream focused on relinquishing judgment and having compassion even for the pedophile.

I am not talking about slapping a person on the wrist for committing acts of violence. I am suggesting we stop promoting false truths. People can change. As a society, we believe that people cannot change and they can if given the right tools. There isn't a behavior that a person cannot change when they learn to change their mind. We are not powerless and as a society we encourage crimes because we support them by believing in a victim mentality.

If a person has the desire to change, they can change. Of course, no one can change if they just attempt to stop the behavior. The behavior is caused by the thoughts and feelings they have about their life. Certain beliefs have to be in place before an act can be committed against another person. There was a professional psychologist on a talk show that suggested that in order for a pedophile to be trusted he would have to have about five years of intensive therapy. In other words, they were encouraging pedophiles to feel hopeless at any recovery. This is the same way alcoholics are treated when it comes to recovery. This whole belief system stems from a victim mentality. They obviously don't know how to help them or they would, without giving them a life sentence.

If you truly knew how to help someone it wouldn't take any longer than teaching him or her how to use the power of his or her mind effectively. First we have to know we are not powerless to change our lives. We are in control of what we allow ourselves to think and feel. We can change limiting thoughts and feelings. We have to start by releasing ourselves from guilt so we can let go of the past and stop recreating it. Guilt is simply fuel for negative behaviors. It allows us to feel negatively about ourselves and encourages feelings of separation and isolation.

There are those who are not willing to change. They are completely happy with their lives even if they are destroying themselves. Some people choose to destroy others along with them. These people are living the consequences of their thoughts every moment. Eventually they will choose to change because they won't be able to tolerate living with themselves any longer.

Guilt torments our minds because the ego cannot control you without it. If someone commits a crime, eventually he/she has to tell someone. It has its benefits in the world of illusion. However, in a world where wholeness is acknowledged, crimes would not be committed against others in thought, word, or deed. Attack in any form doesn't occur because it is a result of the belief in separation. Relinquishing guilt is a process that takes place during the awakening process. It is difficult to release when your world is based on the ego-illusion.

Restructuring your whole thought system is a process that takes place gradually. You would appear rather insane if it took place all at once. The changes would be too dramatic and you wouldn't know how to interpret the information you were receiving. Do you know why the world doesn't make any sense? The thought system of the ego doesn't make sense and the world is based on it. Of course there are many people who are content with their dreaming and do not choose to wake up. They will continue to see through the eyes of their ego rather than the unlimited expression of their self.

Wherever your attention goes, there you are. How can you fully enjoy life if you are in your past? You remain chained to the past through guilt or to future expectations which prevent you from living fully in the present. Many people feel guilt is a necessary emotion that somehow assists them in going beyond their sins. If you feel horrible about what you did and repent, God will forgive you. In truth,

God sees no reason to forgive you because he hasn't condemned you. You were created perfect, whole and complete. It is you who have separated yourself from God and feel guilty about it. *ACIM* explains that you need merely correct your errors. If you learn from your mistakes and let them go, then you can progress in life. If you continue to harbor guilt, you remain chained to your past. You cannot step beyond it unless you learn to forgive yourself. If you are thinking about something you did last night and wish you had reacted differently, where is your attention? It is in the past. You cannot find peace there. It is in the present moment.

The Present

If you are going to climb a mountain, do you enjoy the climb or do you wait until you reach the summit before you are happy? Find joy in the moment. When you are fully present with whatever it is you are doing, you will know peace. The frantic attempt to get somewhere you are not is a state of mind which is in constant conflict with itself. If only this and that were different, then you could be at peace. Changing external circumstances or situations never brings you peace. You will have to be constantly arranging the world to fit within the parameters you have designed for peace. Peace is in the present moment.

I remember a time where I would be coming home from the grocery store, and I would be thinking about putting the groceries away. Apparently I was always in the future in my mind, as if peace were there. By the time I actually got home to put away the groceries, I had done it several times in my mind! I soon found something else to contemplate which needed completion before my mind was at peace.

When I am in the present moment it is as if time stands still. I am unaware of time. Time doesn't really exist; it is an ego-based measurement of reality. Only the ego needs to know what time it is because it bases its state of mind around it. Is it lunchtime yet? If we let our inner guidance direct our actions, we would only eat when we are hungry. Sure enough, time is useful for meeting appointments but it has become a measurement of reality for many people.

The idea of letting go of thoughts of past and future seems difficult to do, but in reality it is far more difficult to hang on to them. The past is gone and cannot be changed. There is no point in dwelling on it or feeling guilty about anything in it. We can learn from things we have done but we should not carry the baggage with us. *"To be born again is to let the past go, and look without condemnation upon the present." (ACIM, I. p.251, 3; 5)*

Fearing the future is also useless. It creates conditions called worry and anxiety. If you stay in the present moment and trust the future will take care of itself, then you create this reality. Fear creates as well as trust. You can put your faith in fear or trust. It is all up to you. The outcome will reflect where you have placed your faith.

The process of discovering our divinity is a rather freeing process. To know that our thoughts create and that our potential is truly unlimited unless we limit it is freedom. Can you spend a day thinking of only higher ideals? How about a moment? See how fast your ego takes over your mind and has it mindlessly wandering with fear and apprehension.

You know your ego is in control when it is thinking about the past or the future. The Holy Spirit is always in the present moment where there is no fear. Spend right now thinking thoughts of joy, peace, is-ness and being, simply for the sake of being without the needs of the ego.

Peace

As a child I can remember seeing the word peace written on a tapestry hanging from the wall of the church. It was just a word to me at the time, but I remember contemplating it in terms of world peace. It was something the world had to experience together, not something I could experience within myself. I remember thinking about the impossibility of the world living in peace. It seemed quite a feat to be accomplished. Of course now I understand the impossibility comes from the desire or need to change other people. Somehow I believed it was other people who needed to change because I was not one of them.

I am now learning what real peace is about. I had to let go of the belief that peace was a state of being that other people needed to achieve towards each other. In truth, it is never about other people. We can only change the world by looking to ourselves. We always see ourselves reflected in the world. Peace is a state of being we can experience for ourselves.

As I got older I began searching for peace without really knowing it. I looked for peace by seeing it in a future state of being; usually after my next drink. I believed it was only available in the future if so and so took place. Peace is in the present moment and it merely needs to be acknowledged instead of denied. Now is the moment to experience your being as God created you. You simply have to let go of any preconceived notions you already have about it. To test your personal belief system, ask yourself, "Has it brought me peace and total acceptance of others and myself?" "Do I love without fear?" "Am I free of judgment?"

In order to experience peace we have to forgive others as ourselves, and let go of judgment, guilt and fear. These are all obstacles to experiencing the peace that is prevalent within our own being. When I recognize "others" as myself, I let go of condemnation and attack. I will not experience the need to control or change other people. I recognize the changes that need to take place are within the perceptions I hold about me.

Judgment is a word often misunderstood. It is indicative of separation and is a direct result of guilt and fear. When I experience anger or guilt in my own being, I will often project it onto others in the form of hostility or resentment. If I keep it to myself, I may experience it in the form of depression, or any other self-defeating thought. It is the belief in separation which creates judgment, and it will disappear when a person realizes wholeness. We are not separate from the judgments we make against others. We separate ourselves from each other when we express judgment or condemnation of any sort because the process splits our mind from theirs. We cannot make judgments without experiencing separation because it is a natural cause and effect.

We can observe a person's behavior without making judgments about it. For instance if I see someone is expressing cruelty, I can take note without labeling it as evil. You would help them more with a blessing then an additional curse. You would also experience the effects of the blessing as opposed to the curse. *"When a brother acts insanely, he is offering you an opportunity to bless him. His need is yours. You need the blessing you can offer him. There is no way for you to have it except by giving it. This is the law of God, and it has no exceptions. (ACIM, I. p.127,2;1-5).*

If I send a person a negative judgment, I experience the effects of those thoughts. There is no way around it; we experience the direct effects of our thoughts. We are responsible to others as well as ourselves when we offer a blessing as opposed to a curse. I am not saying we should sit back and let someone abuse another person or animal. We certainly would need to take the appropriate action to intervene. However, it is our thoughts we need to control in such a circumstance. Attacking the abuser with our thoughts because of their behavior would simply reinforce the anger and hatred they are already feeling within themselves. When we get angry and attack back, we are just like the person we are attacking.

I judge when I know how someone should live their life and anything not in accordance with my ideas, are wrong. We can make observations about other people without judging them right or wrong. For instance people are entitled to limit their expression by fearing God and placing restrictions on their lives. It is a choice they make but it isn't necessarily wrong, just different. Eventually they may tire of the self-imposed limitations and search for freedom as well.

Many people believe the Last Judgment refers to a process that occurs after death. *"The Last Judgment is generally thought of as a procedure undertaken by God. Actually it will be undertaken by my brothers with my help. It is a final healing rather than a meting out of punishment, however much you think that punishment is deserved. Punishment is a concept totally opposed to right-mindedness, and the aim of the Last Judgment is to restore right-mindedness to you. The Last Judgment might be called a process of right evaluation." (ACIM, I. p.34,3;1-5)*

Along with the acceptance of unity, you will experience the last judgment because it will no longer be necessary. Judgment can only exist in a mind that judges against itself as an imperfect creation of God. When your mind is restored to the awareness of perfect oneness, judgment ceases to exist in your mind. *"The term "Last Judgment" is frightening, not only because it has been projected onto God, but also because of the association of "last" with death. This is an outstanding example of upside-down perception. If the meaning of the Last Judgment is objectively examined, it is quite apparent that it is really the doorway to life."(ACIM, I. p.35,5;1-3)* People fear the last judgment along with every other fearful interpretation of God's word. If God created life so that you could live it only to be condemned in the end, it certainly wouldn't say much about God. This is a contradiction of what I know to be true. The love of God would not create anything unlike itself. The magnificent power of creation creates in its own image. It is simply a violation of natural laws for this not to be true.

Peace comes with the acceptance of your being as it was intended. Whenever you sway your attention to experiences you perceive as threatening, you are identifying with your ego. Your true identity cannot be threatened. Peace can be experienced now. A mind in the past or future cannot be in the presence of peace. Learn to live in the now. It is the only time that exists anyhow.

Your awareness encompasses everything and everyone around you. In truth there is nothing that exists outside of you. *"The word "within" is really unnecessary. The Kingdom of heaven is you. What else but you did the Creator create, and what else but you is His Kingdom?"(ACIM, I. p.60,1; 3-5)* You perceive through your own eyes. The ego perceives through the collection of your past experiences which become the window through which you look. The window becomes clouded when you use the past to judge the present. You cannot free the future to experience freedom unless you forgive your own past.

How often do you reminisce about the past in terms of fond

memories? All too frequently you use the past against yourself by remembering events, people or situations, which are painful or guilt-ridden. Even when you reminisce about fond memories you are missing the moment because your focus is in the past.

In order to free yourself from the constraints of the ego, you need to practice quieting your mind. Listening to your Spirit requires a quiet mind and a willingness to quiet the ego's rather riotous voice. With practice it will become as natural to listen to Spirit, as it is now to listen to your ego. At first light, I would suggest spending time quieting the mind and aligning yourself with Spirit. It is important to take the time at the beginning of the day, leaving your Spirit in charge rather than your ego. The end of the day is a good time to spend quieting the mind as well. A few moments of gratitude are also refreshing and it enables you to align your thoughts with higher ideals. Any time throughout the day when you feel yourself connecting with fear, it is always a good time to quiet your mind and re-align your thinking with peace.

When you learn to quiet your mind and go within, a new world is revealed. It is the most important thing you can do for yourself. People may fear quieting their mind as with everything else in their life. Fear can creep in at the most inopportune times, because its very life is threatened. Indeed, fear itself is threatened once a person discovers their true identity. Fear, ego, separation, and judgment are all terms linked in the description of the fall, or the moment we lost touch with our true identity.

Reconnecting with our Spirit takes discipline and effort. We have to be willing to do what it takes to free ourselves from the wrath of the ego. All we need to do is let go of everything in the way of experiencing peace. Going within, ultimately refers to the joining of our Spirit with our mind and body. They have never really been separate but our perception of it has made it a reality. Mind, body and Spirit are one and only the ego would consider them separately.

Healing

Healing takes place in the present moment. It is never about the past in any form. *"Healing cannot be accomplished in the past. It must be accomplished in the present to release the future." (ACIM. I. p.247, 9; 3 and 4)* Some people believe they need to go into the past to find release from pain and to create healing. It is only in the present that you can create change. You are not at the mercy of past lives or past experiences or anything other than the false perceptions you hold about yourself in the present. A therapist doesn't need to take you into your past to discover your psychological troubles; they merely need to assist you in releasing your mind in the present.

True healing cannot occur until you have healed your belief in separation from God. Jesus knew he was not separate from God and he was trying to teach us the same thing. Indeed we need saving; saving from the self we created. I know God created us perfect. We have created imperfection out of perfection. We have taken the power of creation and turned it against ourselves. Upon entering the physical world, we lost touch with our essence and the power inherent in each of us.

It is time for us to regain our personal power. We have misplaced it in the form of addictions, diseases and disorders. The list includes any effect, caused from a belief in separation. Hatred, jealousy, and envy, are just a few examples of feelings that result from the belief in separation. A person experiencing these emotions doesn't believe they have the power to create whatever it is they feel they are lacking.

Illness is created through a thought system which believes in fear. Every emotion you experience directly affects the body your energy encompasses. From the very moment of conception, your energy system takes inventory of the thoughts and feelings surrounding you. Oftentimes you identify with surrounding emotions and lose sight of your own.

An example would be a home where obesity is prevalent. Do the children inherit the obese gene, or do they succumb to the thoughts and feelings that surround them and support the behavior leading to obesity? In some instances, there is one child who refuses to become obese. They deny the participation in linking their energy system with the collective attitude in their family.

I saw a television program the other night, which discussed the problems with obesity. It singled out a particular Indian tribe and it said they were among the most obese people in the country. They suggested this was proof that genetics plays a role in obesity. I would have to argue the point. It only proves they share the same thought system. If genetics plays such a significant role, then we would have to be victims of our bodies and I know this is not true. It may be true in a world of dreams but not in truth.

It could be they are still living in their past and feeding their own pain with food. Their focus may still be on the idea that they are victims of their past rather than letting it go and creating a new future. It is very possible. I am not undermining their experience, but just the belief that they have to be victims for the remainder of their lives. Whenever you are focusing on a group of people and the similar experiences they share, you are talking about a collective attitude or thought system. Of course this is just an example so it may or may not be true.

As a young child, I saw all my family members get glasses. I remember the day I made a conscious decision to always have perfect eyesight. Well, today I am thirty-eight years old and I still have perfect vision. Everyone else in the family including my adopted brother had to have glasses.

Healing our sense of separation from God restores perfect health. We have never been separate from God but we believe we are, and therefore experience the effects of this belief. There are many different illnesses with many symptoms, but the cause is the same. There seem to be many ways to heal these illnesses but there is only one. God is at work behind the healing of any disease or illness. Faith may be placed in many different types of healing methods but it is always the love of God that restores health. I can place my faith in a pill to heal me but in my opinion it is the faith that heals, and not the pill.

I remember reading an article about multiple personality disorder and it discussed one personality as having an allergy to a certain type of food. The other personality didn't have the allergy. If the person switched personalities in the midst of an allergic reaction, the symptoms would disappear. This says a lot to me about the power of our minds. The body remained the same; it was their mind, which changed. If we look around us we will find many examples that lead us to explanations regarding the power of belief and the effects on our bodies.

According to "experts", there is a connection between the mind and the body. Placebo is used as a control substance to determine the effects of a natural substance on the body in comparison to the experimental medication. They use it to account for the side effects of a natural substance on the body. In other words, it is used to discount the power of the mind to test the effects of their experimental drug on the body.

It isn't possible to have an effect on the body that isn't caused in the mind. The body experiences the effects of the mind and there is no in between. A person's belief system needs to be examined in order to discover what will or will not work for someone in regards to recovery. There are many different methods of healing because everyone differs in their thoughts, beliefs and ideas about healing.

Conventional healing, whether it is in modern or alternative medicine, is only temporary. True healing only needs to be accomplished once. When the mind is at one with God, it can only experience wholeness. A mind that thinks it is separate from God will experience intermittent periods of illness. Faith in illness is enough to encourage its reoccurrence, predicating the person's belief in vulnerability.

Simply stated, the vulnerability of a person to disease or illness of any kind is equal to their belief in its possibility. Fear itself can create illness. If you have faith in the threat of an illness your faith will be rewarded. Faith in healing is the same. We can choose fear or love, sickness or health.

A COURSE IN MIRACLES explains that illness is a decision we make. After examining my own thoughts and their effects, I have to agree. I have suffered from the affliction of cold sores since I was about eighteen years old. I remember a time when I would be just devastated when an outbreak occurred. I was so worried about the way I looked and a cold sore was a sight for sore eyes. I would get huge cold sores on my nose and chin and other odd places. They say a lot of people have cold sores regularly, but I seemed like the only one. Anyhow, I spent a greater part of my life trying to prevent them from occurring. I would come across different methods to cure or prevent them and sometimes I would have an instantaneous healing. I tried many different remedies and each one seemed to work once or twice and that would be it. I had to keep changing the substance in order to treat them. I knew for a long time that the cure wasn't "out there" and neither was the cause.

Then one day it occurred to me, that there was something I needed to learn from them. Several thoughts came to mind. I realized that the more I resisted them, the more often they would occur. What you resist will persist. But how do you keep from resisting them? I had to decide that it simply didn't matter one way or the other, and let go of the fear. If I was going to keep getting cold sores no matter what I did, then why not succumb and just let it go? After all, the cold sores bothered me because they were not very nice to look at, not to mention the social implications. Nevertheless, I decided to let go of the importance that I had attached to them. I began to review my thoughts from the day before the outbreak and realized I made a mental note regarding the next occurrence and expected frequency. Mind you, I also had faith in this belief or they wouldn't reoccur.

The last experience I had with an outbreak was an awakening

experience. I awoke one morning to experience the pain and redness often associated with an outbreak. Instead of reacting as if it would get worse and attaching fear to it in any way, I chose to let it go. I said to myself, "Just because it looks real and the normal outcome is a big red cold sore on my nose, I let it go." I decided not to put any energy in it whatsoever by giving it any attention. Later on in the day I happened to look in the mirror and to my amazement, it was gone. When I had first looked at it, it was painful and I could tell it was going to be a real good sore based on all of my past experiences. We can choose whether or not we need to make something real or not. *"If God created you perfect, you are perfect. If you believe you can be sick, you have placed other gods before Him. God is not at war with the god of sickness you made, but you are. He is the symbol of deciding against God, and you are afraid of him because he can not be reconciled with God's Will. If you attack him, you will make him real to you. But if you refuse to worship him in whatever form he may appear to you, and wherever you think you see him, he will disappear into the nothingness out of which he was made." (ACIM, I. p.187, 1; 4-9)*

There are times when I slip back into the old habit of fear expecting a cold sore and my faith is rewarded. I noticed that I always have the thought first and when it is linked with fear, I experience the effects. Letting go of fear is a process that takes persistence but with the help of our Spirit we can overcome our challenges. I sometimes have to wonder that if I never viewed the film in high school they showed on herpes, would my experience have been different. I remember the fear I had about getting the ugly sores they showed on the film. It wasn't long after this that I had my first experience.

We are told there is no cure for herpes. Unfortunately, we believe it. We place our faith in what science tells us is the truth and sure enough it proves itself true. There isn't an illness on earth that isn't curable. Every illness has something to tell us about ourselves, including our thoughts and beliefs. We need to stop focusing on stopping the symptoms of illness and recognize them as a signal we need to pay attention to in order to change the thoughts and beliefs we hold. What we are thinking and believing is where we need to make the changes in our lives. Our body will respond and symptoms will disappear.

When we learn to recognize fear in its most disguised forms, we can let it go. We have spent years responding to external events with fear and it takes time to learn new ways to respond to the world. A COURSE IN MIRACLES states that illness is a defense against the truth. Sure enough, I find myself questioning what I know to be true whenever I do become ill. Once again I feel out of control and a victim of my body. *"The body can act wrongly only when it is responding to misthought. The body cannot create, and the belief that it can, a fundamental error, produces all physical symptoms."* (ACIM, I. P.23, 2: 5,6)

Absolute health is a state of mind that can only be reached when it is seen as whole. A separate mind has within it the seeds for destruction. Separation itself is a thought system that cannot be reconciled. It never really makes any sense, and people continue to seek for answers where they cannot find them. The thought system of the world is backwards. If we look to the world for answers, we will only find illusions. The world itself is an illusion. Sure it seems real enough, for we have made it so.

What really matters in this world of illusion is the love which connects us together. We need to discover this love as a part of us. Love is what we are. In the world of illusion, love is what you give and receive from another. In actuality, love IS and it is either expressed or it is not.

I know and feel the love that I am when I see my children. One of the first times I ever felt love within, was when I became a mother. My children have assisted me in knowing and recognizing the love within myself. I know that I recognize the love in them only to the degree in which I know it in myself. My parents always shared their love with me but I didn't always know it was a part of me. I am thankful for the power to express and experience this love now. I know I have greater levels of awareness to achieve and this will enable me to experience love even more deeply.

Love is omnipresent, and we have to let go of every thought, idea and belief that gets in the way of its expression. We are all love. We have hidden it through fear, guilt, judgment and condemnation. We are all endowed with the power to create through fear or love. Anger is a good indicator we are using fear against others and ourselves.

I was attending a non-denominational church one day and the minister spoke of the devil. He was talking about casting away the sins of the devil as if there was some other force responsible for our wrongdoings. How can we do anything to change what we do not like about ourselves, if someone else is responsible? We are responsible for the thoughts we think and the behaviors we follow. When we align ourselves with the Holy Spirit, there will not be a need to monitor our behavior. We will not sin against others or ourselves because we will not use guilt, judgment and condemnation to strengthen our belief in it.

I read a billboard one day in front of a church that said, "forbidden fruit creates many jams". The notion was that when you do things wrong, you get a lot of problems. I feel that the very idea of forbidding something through fear makes it seem more enticing to some people. Look at the sexual hang-ups in this country. People fear sex and create all kinds of laws, rules and regulations against it. People feel sinful about it and hence, all kinds of disorders result. The only thing sinful about our bodies is when their purpose is used for separation. When we allow the Holy Spirit to guide our life, we feel whole once again without the need or use for fear.

In conclusion, I would have to say the answers can only be found within. The world itself is a contradiction leaving little room for true health and healing. There is a place within where only love exists. In this space of knowingness and love, there is no such thing as sickness or death, only eternal life.

Safety

The keys to the kingdom have never left you. You may have forgotten where you hid them but nevertheless, they are with you. It only requires an intense desire to find them. You have to be as intent to find the keys as you have been in misplacing them. Your focus has to switch to your personal freedom rather than bondage.

You have instilled your faith in safety in irrational yet mysterious ways. You believe safety comes from controlling the outside world. When you truly know yourself, safety is not a concern. There is nothing that can harm the Son of God who has recognized truth.

Years ago, I had an experience with my dear sister I will never forget. I am glad she was there to share it with me. I may not have believed it myself if she hadn't experienced it too. On this particular occasion my sister and I were driving home from a pub. We had only had one drink and I had only finished half of mine. We decided we were both tired and we wanted to go home. I was driving home and I slowed down because we were coming to an intersection. The lights turned green so we didn't have to stop. We were about half way into the intersection when we saw a car coming at us at about 45 miles per hour. The speed limit in the area was only about 25 mph. Apparently, the person was trying to beat the light. I remember thinking to myself oh no, they are going to kill my sister. I had absolutely no thoughts about my own safety. All of a sudden I put my foot on the gas and found myself driving up the hill. To this day, we don't know what happened to the other car. It was only a few feet away from hitting us when it disappeared. We both looked back and it was gone. We thought for sure it would have interrupted traffic on the other side, but there was nothing. We were both stunned.

I have always felt safe. I never questioned it; it was just something I always knew. I know my parents had a lot to do with it. They always helped me feel safe and they believed in the power of God. As a young child, when I was scared of something in the closet, they would tell me to say, "in the name of Jesus, go away." I always knew this would keep me safe and it has many times.

When you know you are safe, there is nothing that can harm you. If you learn to listen to inner guidance, it will always tell you what you need to do to stay safe. One day, I was stopped at a stop sign and I turned around and handed something to my son. A voice told me to be sure to check both ways again. I turned around and gently put my foot on the gas to turn. Thankfully, I heeded the advice. A car came out of nowhere and sped right by me. Had I not listened, we could have been injured.

In actuality it wasn't a voice but a thought. It was a loud thought and I knew it was important to listen. Many times I have heard it referred to as a still small voice. I think it can actually be very loud when we pay attention to it. I remember when I used to override this voice because I didn't know how to recognize it. I am thankful I am able to listen now.

I have had many instances in the car where I have been saved from near accidents. There is one time I will always remember. I had been to visit a friend in Iowa and on the way home I got a little lost. I didn't always listen to my feelings back then and I went the wrong way for a long time. Anyhow, I was tired and frustrated by the end of the day. I went off one of the Rockford exits so I could use the restroom. Apparently, there was no direct route back onto the highway. The woman at the gas station thought it was funny to give me the wrong directions and I ended up in the middle of nowhere. I turned around and headed back toward the city. I ended up in Rockford in a not so cool part of town. Of course, I didn't know this because I was quite naïve. I stopped at a fast food joint to ask for directions back onto the highway. I walked in and realized I was not in a friendly place. There were men sitting at a table drinking and the woman that worked there asked them to help me out. I turned to walk out and got right in my car. I locked the door and rolled up the window. A man followed me out and tried to get in the car with me. Thank God a voice told me to lock the passenger door before I went into the store. Every now and then I think about that event and what could have happened. I soon realize I need to focus on gratefulness, rather then fear.

Speaking of safety, I guess I need to make an important point. A home security person was just here trying to sell me a system to keep me safe. I know I am safe, so it would be kind of silly for me to have a security system. The man suggested that I get the system before we are burglarized rather than afterwards. I guess this man's job is to spread fear so he can sell his security system.

If I am a victim in a world of separate minds and separate bodies, surely I need security systems to protect me because then I am always in fear and in need of protection. Perhaps I need a gun to feel safe or locks and chains on my doors. Safety can be reached by recognizing the power inherent in us. It is a state of being that doesn't recognize fear. It is a knowingness that emanates through the mind which creates a state of being reflecting peace and security.

I remember a time when I lived at home with my parents and their neighborhood was burglarized. Several homes right behind ours were burglarized and the burglars were even in our back yard. They left checkbooks and other remnants behind. They never broke into our home and I know one of the doors was even left open. The next day a police officer stopped at our home to ask us if our home was burglarized as well. Are we vulnerable to outside influences or do we have to believe we are in order to experience that reality?

There was a time when my husband and I were saved from a fire. I woke up in the middle of the night and I smelled smoke. I walked around the house and everything seemed in order. There was a towel rack in the bathroom and it was above a space heater in the wall. Obviously we never turned it on. Somehow the space heater got turned on and there was a towel hanging there. The towel was smoldering and would have caught the house on fire if I hadn't awakened when I did. I know there was divine intervention here.

On one occasion, we received a notice in the mail concerning a ten-year furnace inspection. Apparently the gas company does this every ten years. We had just bought a home about a year and a half prior to receiving this notice. It was the first time we had owned a home and we were not familiar with regular furnace inspections. Thankfully, out of the blue we received this notice. The man came by and checked our furnace on a Friday. He commented that it needed cleaning really badly and that we needed to turn it off immediately before it went through the roof. He said we might have not made it through the weekend by the looks of it. Our home had been a rental home and apparently not well taken care of before we bought it. Thank God we were due for a ten-year inspection. I don't believe in coincidences or I may have brushed this incident off as luck. It was sincerely a blessing.

Since I began writing about safety, God has shown me a few instances that have only made my faith stronger. The first was a near miss accident involving my daughter. My husband was in the attic drilling holes for speaker wires. My son was helping him with the tools. My husband handed him the drill at one point. It came apart and he dropped the drill. The drill weighed at least fifteen pounds. My daughter had just gone out to the garage to see what they were doing. She started up the attic stairs. I went out to the garage at the same moment I heard a crash. I thought my son was falling or something. I saw Kayla standing on the stairs at the same moment I saw the drill fall from the attic door space. I saw it fall in slow motion and I stood there and said, "Do not hit Kayla." It bounced off a rung on the ladder. Kayla had started down the stairs when she heard the crash. I yelled, "watch out!" as the drill bounced off the rung and went flying through the air. She ducked at the exact moment she needed to in order to avoid the drill for the second time. It landed right next to her and a piece flew off and was thrown about thirty feet through the garage door. Thank God the garage door was open or it would have ricocheted again. The event was perfectly orchestrated in that it kept Kayla safe. She had a little scratch on her cheek and that was it.

At first, fear pervaded my mind. I thought about the "what-ifs" surrounding the event. Then my husband commented we should be thankful and let it go. I had to agree with him. I was extremely thankful. I remember asking myself "why didn't I do anything?" The event was already in motion when I went out to the garage but I wondered why I didn't do anything. In actuality, prayer felt like my only choice in the moment. I felt no body awareness as I was focused on the drill avoiding Kayla. Doing something was simply not a choice. The event was already in motion but as time stood still it seemed like I could have done something. I am glad the thought never occurred to me because it would have been interference. At this moment she was in God's care. Thank God.

The next instance where safety was a concern was a terrible storm that left us without power for two days. Some people lost their homes and someone was even killed. Tornadoes were touching down all around us, for an eight-hour period. I connected with my spirit during this time and I felt completely peaceful.

It seems there have been many instances in my life where I could have been injured or killed. Many of us have had close calls. I know we have all asked ourselves the question, why did this have to happen to me? In the instance where someone loses a loved one through a tragic experience, there are many explanations which try to make it easier on the survivors. We all have to wonder why some of us survive and some of us do not. I know it isn't because any of us are more important than anyone else. I know the ego would define it quite differently than the Holy Spirit. The ego would explain it in terms of fear, guilt and judgment.

Who is in control of the decision when it comes to death? I am sure everyone is curious about this as well. Some people believe God is in charge of this decision and we have no control over it. It seems that people are saved from near death because it isn't their time yet, while for others it is. So what determines when it is a person's time? Maybe if we knew the answers to these questions, we think it would interfere with our ability to live fully. Some people may have a fear that if they accomplish so and so, then it is their time to cross over.

I am not sure it is not about that at all. If we believe the physical experience is a school where we identify ourselves as students, I suppose when we graduate we die. What if death isn't a diploma at all? What if it is about something as simple as a misperception? Maybe some of us think we will be happier when we are not in a physical world. When our physical self dies, there we are. It is not like death is the great escape from our self, and all of a sudden we have this abundance of knowledge we didn't have before. Of course, we may be enlightened in one sense because we will not have a body to limit us. Maybe life is simply about discovering our own divinity? Everyone has his own idea and experiences their life around this central theme of existence.

People believe there is divine timing involved in the moment of life or death. Divine timing is a part of life's perfectly orchestrated plan. Some say everyone has a choice when it comes to death. I know this is true. If life and death are ego terms, then certainly transitions are unnecessary. But for many of us, this is too big a leap in faith. After all, death happens all around us reinforcing our existing beliefs. We continue to believe we are victims of our own mind and decisions about our life are not our choice.

Many people who have had near death experiences talk about experiencing the light and an enormous sense of peace and love. It is not necessary to die to have this experience. So much is attributed to death, even knowledge, as if somehow death is the great doorway to freedom. *"When your body and your ego and your dreams are gone, you will know that you will last forever. Perhaps you think this is accomplished through death, but nothing is accomplished through death, because death is nothing. Everything is accomplished through life, and life is of the mind and in the mind."(ACIM, I. p.104, 1; 1-3).*

The Holy Spirit may not recognize death at all. It is the ego that created the body and made it susceptible to outside influences. According to *A COURSE IN MIRACLES*, the body doesn't even exist in the present moment. It says that the body is either remembered or anticipated. I experienced this very notion when I had moments without body awareness. Following my experiences, I had a renewed sense of myself. I now see my body as an extension of myself rather than who I am.

"*Safety is the complete relinquishment of attack.*" *(ACIM, I. p.100, 3; 7)* We cannot experience attack in our "external" world if it is not a part of our thoughts and beliefs. In order to fear attack, I have to believe in attack. If I no longer attack others in my mind, then I simply share and extend perfect peace. Attacking produces fear in others including a simple expression of anger. When I attack with anger, what happens to the person receiving it? They feel the anger and often attack back as a natural response. Attack creates more attack unless you can learn to free your mind from responding to it. You change how people respond to you when you change how you treat them with your thoughts.

If I am whole then safety is not a concern. I have no reason to fear. My mind is at peace. When I create from a peaceful existence, fear cannot enter my mind because it is simply denied power. I have to wonder, what would a world be like without fear? Paradise is probably a good description. Is it possible to achieve this on earth? I know that as I become more and more aware, feelings of fear are becoming less predominant. I know paradise can be achieved on earth and I intend to recognize this state of being.

I recently saw a movie where the people were caught in these cubes. If they left one room they would simply go into another room identical to the one they were in. They had multiple selves living in this multi-dimensional cube. It is a bit like releasing ourselves from the constraints of the ego. It literally has us locked into seeing the world in a certain way. One woman finally made it out of the cube when it imploded upon itself. She figured out how to survive by jumping through the center. It turned out to be a government experiment and after she made it out of the cube alive she was shot and killed. The ego has us convinced that we will be killed if we release ourselves from its grip as well. We think that the death of the ego is the death of ourselves but the opposite is actually true. Releasing ourselves from the ego- based illusion of reality frees us from death through the recognition of our eternal self.

I had a dream one night that was nothing short of horrifying. My son was in the hospital and my husband was saying that he was going to be killed and brought back to life again. To think that a father would have you experience death over and over again in order to heal you is completely insane. I truly related this dream to the teachings of A COURSE IN MIRACLES. I wouldn't put my son through this experience anymore then God would want to put us through it. We live life after life and continue to experience death simply because we haven't escaped the ego's thought system. It is the ego that created death, not God. Can you imagine doing that to your own children? To kill them and then bring them back to life, merely to experience pain and suffering once again?

I know this is completely difficult to swallow, but it is merely introducing the idea that we have created pain and suffering, not God. We can open our minds to the possibility that even death can be transcended. It may be difficult to simply relinquish this belief because death surrounds us everywhere. Simply be open to another interpretation of life. Transitions are really unnecessary and we can free our minds from the need to experience them.

I haven't yet released my own mind from the belief in death but I can tell you I know it is possible. I know that it makes sense to me that God wouldn't create a world where pain and death occurs. I understand how we lost ourselves in the physical reality. I understand how we forgot who we are as well. It makes perfect sense. What doesn't make sense is the world we have created. To release ourselves from the hatred and fear that encompasses this world, we need to acknowledge our divinity and focus on love rather than fear.

Vision

If we look in the mirror and see our reflection as who we are, then we are not seeing truth. We are merely seeing an image. Who we are cannot be seen with physical eyes. The body is a limitation and if we place our faith in it, then we are stuck with controlling the physical in order to feel in control or at peace.

My Spirit revealed to me the meaning of real vision while I was sitting in a doctor's office one day. I was sitting there reading the posters on the wall. All of a sudden I felt a powerful presence surround me. I felt safe and peaceful so I wasn't afraid. For a few moments, I thought there was something wrong with my eyes. Things began to disappear. Letters in the middle of words would just disappear. I had always had perfect vision so it was rather mysterious. I could hear my children playing and I knew they were there, but for a few moments I couldn't see them. I got up to go to the bathroom. I opened the door and looked in the mirror. To my surprise I could only see half of my face. I have to say I was rather relieved when my sight was restored to normal; although I never quite saw things the same again. I learned a lot that day about the power of God and real vision. *"The real beauty of the temple cannot be seen with the physical eye. Spiritual sight, on the other hand, cannot see the structure at all because it is perfect vision."(ACIM, I. p.21,1; 10)*

I have had this experience several times since the first occurrence. The subsequent episodes have not been as shocking as the first one. They may serve simply as a reminder of what is real and what is not. Of course I questioned whether or not this was a spiritual experience at all. I thought maybe I was having periods of unexplained blind spots or something. I went to the doctor and had him check my eyes. He said maybe I had moments where my blood pressure dropped real low or something. He thought it was pretty weird also. Needless to say, he couldn't find anything wrong with my eyes.

I decided to go to an ophthalmologist and get a full visual exam. A part of me knew it was a spiritual experience while the other part had concerns. I wanted to know for sure that it wasn't a medical problem that needed attention. The doctor told me I had 20/20 vision and very healthy eyes. He said there were no known medical explanations for my experiences and he said they were what they called unexplained visual phenomena. Medical science cannot explain my experiences so that was good enough proof for me. Since I have been to the eye doctor and had my fears alleviated, the episodes have not reoccurred.

On a couple of occasions, I experienced a state in which I had brief periods without body awareness. It left me with a knowingness that cannot really be explained in words. The first time, I was on a walk with my children and my parents. We were walking around a golf course and there were some people playing golf. We stopped to wait for them to swing, so we would not get struck with a golf ball. The thought was to stand back and wait. Suddenly, I saw everything at what I thought was a subatomic level. The road was moving towards us as if to keep us "standing back". I saw every particle in motion. I was in a state of pure consciousness and had no body awareness whatsoever. I remember wanting to stay in the presence of this vision and keep fear at bay so that I could do so. Nevertheless, it lasted only moments. I remember saying, "wow!" I then continued to try and explain what had just happened to me.

On the second occasion where I had moments without body awareness, I was at the beach. My daughter and I were standing at the shore. She was only about eight months old. She fell down and before I knew it, she was under water. I was standing right there, so I reached down to grab her. As I reached down, it was like time stood still. For a moment I was pure consciousness meeting pure consciousness. Normally, I would have been scared for my daughter because the water was murky and I couldn't see her. I felt this reassuring presence and a peace that I know she shared with me. She never even cried. We were one.

This is an experience you have to have in order to understand. I know it was real and many people may think I am a little weird but that is okay. Thankfully, I don't need your belief to validate my experience. People think they have to see things with their eyes for them to be true. This is a misperception. Take hypnosis for example. A hypnotist can convince you something is there, when it really isn't. Your mind has been convinced of a reality that the audience does not share with you. Is either of them really real?

I remember seeing a hypnotist convince a man he was looking at a celebrity. The man really thought the hypnotist was someone else. A hypnotist can also convince a man he has abilities he doesn't really think he has. So where is the mind? It is not just limited to a body. It is everywhere.

So what if this world really isn't real? That it is only in place as a manifestation of our thoughts and beliefs. Everything only appears to be solid because we have agreed to see it this way. Do you know the implications of this? When you actually get over it, it is quite a freeing feeling. I know one thing for sure. Your thoughts alter this "reality". It is time to get control of our thoughts and stop letting them control us.

Our reality changes as we free ourselves from limiting beliefs. Beliefs can imprison our mind. Freedom comes when we let go and let the Holy Spirit guide our vision. Then we are free to truly live as God created us to be. We are then free of the restrictions and limitations we have imposed upon ourselves. Could it be that we are limited only by our choice? Could it be that we choose to refuse our true identity out of fear? What are we afraid of? What could possibly be more fearful than the world the ego created?

We have long since forgotten a place within ourselves where there is perfect peace. We have projected this peace outside of our own beings, making it impossible to attain. Peace, love and boundless joy are to be a part of a God outside of you. We ascertain we can only experience this state in a place after death in a place called heaven. We think that we must make up for all of our wrongdoings for we view ourselves as sinners in a world, long gone astray.

Placing authority in a power outside of you has become a customary practice. For eons, man has been worshiping other beings, and placing other Gods before Himself. He has separated himself from the divine creation which created him; all in the name of the very God they deny themselves the power of knowing. When we come to know ourselves, we come to know God.

Salvation can be attained most effortlessly. Salvation already exists and is awaiting the return of each soul, to the acknowledgement of their perfect unity with all of creation. It is not something you have to accomplish for it is already done. You simply have to remove the impediments to the realization of your true self.

Guilt, judgment and fear, are guards to the gates of freedom. As long as you hold on to guilt, you project anger and fear onto others. It is your own feelings of guilt which cause you to condemn others. You condemn them in the same way with which you displace all of your feelings. Such is a world filled with hatred and fear. You fear the love within yourself in the form of guilt and shame. Feelings of unworthiness are rampant, spreading like wildfire through the connected minds which share them.

For so long man has been like a puppet. The strings were believed to be pulled by a force outside of him, never knowing what fate was to be handed. Are we at the mercy of an outside force which ultimately controls our destiny? If so, then what is our purpose here? If someone is controlling our destiny and everything is pre-planned, then I would have to ask, "What for?"

I have always questioned everything in my life. The more I learn and discover about myself, the more I know there is to learn. At this point in my life, I know life is learning about the love I am. As I learn to love myself and let go of doubts and fears about who I am, I discover a new world. I discover a world that is in place as a reflection of the new me. It is a different world because I have changed my view of it. I am seeing love all around me. When I look into your eyes, I see love. I am seeing through the lens of love that I know within myself.

Whenever I do not see love within another, I know I do not love myself. I am seeing something in another that I do not like about me. To make any real changes in our lives, we have to change the way we see ourselves. We have to get in touch with the love that is within us. It is my understanding that when we see through the eyes of God, we will see only love.

We are only capable of loving others to the degree with which we love ourselves. We have to be self-full, in order to be able to give fully of ourselves to others. Begin by asking yourself, "What brings me joy?" Whatever makes your heart soar is what you might consider doing with your life. Honor yourself by doing what you love. If you are not presently in a position to do what you love for a living, then start by taking the time to do it for fun. You will begin to connect with the peace within yourself by acknowledging your spirit and doing what brings you joy.

When you know peace within, you will see it around you. I know whenever I am agitated; I also see it reflected in those around me. We are all connected and we affect each other through our thoughts and feelings. To change the world, change the way you view it. *"What would you see? The choice is given you. But learn and do not let your mind forget this law of seeing: You will look upon that which you feel within. If hatred finds a place within your heart, you will perceive a fearful world, held cruelly in death's sharp-pointed, bony fingers. If you feel the Love of God within you, you will look out on a world of mercy and of love". (ACIM, II. p.359,5;1-5)* We come to realize the world we experience is a direct reflection of ourselves, and the thoughts we allow ourselves to think and feel about life. We feel a need for safety when we project fear outside of ourselves as well. At a moment's notice, you can see through the eyes of love. Be willing to have the shades removed from your eyes. The Holy Spirit will do the rest.

The Power of the Mind

We create our own reality and the thoughts we think directly reflect it. Let's say I have misplaced something and I need to find it. I used to walk around the house looking for the object thinking, "I can't find it." That is exactly what I would get. Now I ask, "Where are my sunglasses?" I expect an answer and *viola*; I get a picture in my mind of where to find them. If we tell ourselves beforehand that we cannot do something then that will be our experience. Ask and you shall receive.

My son was having some trouble on his tests in first grade. We reviewed his reading words over and over again and he still managed to get a lot wrong on his tests. One week I decided we would work twice as hard and we did, but to no avail. He still had trouble with his test. Then I posed the question to my higher self. I asked, "What can I do to help Michael?" Immediately I received an answer. He was simply having self-doubt. When we sat down the next night to do his homework I told him to acknowledge the power of his own mind. I suggested he get rid of any negative thoughts such as I don't know and I can't. I explained that I knew he was very smart and that he could learn this easily and effortlessly as soon as he eliminated the self-doubt. I suggested he repeat the words "I know" and I explained the power behind those words. If you tell yourself "I don't know," you close yourself off to knowing. It worked like a charm. Immediately he began reading the words without any trouble. On his next test he got them all right! Now Michael understands about the power of his own mind and the power behind "I know."

I think of all of those children who have trouble in school and all because of their negative self-talk. If they get punished from their parents for not doing well no matter how hard they try, it just makes it worse. Now they are fearful of failing and it only adds fuel to the fire.

Look around you and you will know the thoughts you think as well. Like Jesus said, "By their fruits you shall know them." The life you have created was first done with a thought. If there is something you would like to change the power is yours, you just have to know it. Stop giving your power away to thoughts of limitation and doubt. Accept it as real and it becomes a reality. The only limitation that exists is the limitation in your mind.

So many people attribute the gifts in their life to a God outside of themselves. In reality, you have created it through belief. No doubt a God created you, but you were given the power of creation as well. You have yourself to thank for what is or is not a part of your life. When you have created lack and limitation you cannot blame a force outside of our own beings. You choose whether or not to allow the power of God to manifest in your life. When you let go of limiting and restricting beliefs, you allow good to flow into your life with ease and effortlessness. If you put the focus on a God outside of your own being, you will never come to know yourself. It is through coming to know yourself that you will truly understand the God who created you.

There are so many examples of the power of the mind and it is important to recognize them so that people can change the way they think and experience their life. We create through desire. Never stifle a desire with fear because it simply creates itself. I would not be able to write this book if I allowed fear to keep me from expressing my thoughts. In order to achieve my goal I have to see it in my mind as a possibility. I have to erase doubt through a thought of completion. I have to first recognize the doubt in whatever form it appears, and then change it with the power of my thoughts.

I choose to think the thoughts I would like to experience. For instance, I recently had a thought about not having anything more to say. My writing came to a halt. I stopped and thought of myself writing continuously without any difficulty. Immediately, I began to write and the thoughts have continued to flow without interruption.

Pain is experienced in the body in the same manner. There aren't different degrees of pain tolerance, just different thoughts about it. I can experience pain in my body just by thinking about it. Disease is created in the same manner. A blockage of energy occurs, through thought, and the person focuses their attention upon it. If the attention is centered on an area long enough and if it is coupled with fear, disease is the result. Our thoughts create and we need to release fear so we can create the life we were designed to live.

I remember the pain I experienced with the birth of our first child. After six hours of labor pain they discovered he was breach. When I knew they had to remove him surgically, I felt relieved. For some reason, I feared the pain of natural childbirth more than going under the knife. I suppose it is because there is so much pain associated with it. Six hours of labor pain was enough for me. I have to wonder if we have so much pain with childbirth because we expect it.

I recovered from surgery in direct proportion to my thoughts about it. I remember experiencing a lot of pain after the surgery. I was given pretty strong pain medication and it would put me right to sleep. I didn't see much of my son for the first two days because I was so doped up.

I had a c-section with my daughter as well. I recovered much quicker and had less pain. They gave me half the dose of pain medicine and I really didn't experience a lot of pain. In one week I could sit up using my stomach muscles. Recovery was much quicker because I had changed my mind about it. I readily observed the difference in my mind between the two c-sections because it was so astounding. It was neat to realize the power of my own mind in creating pain and initiating healing.

The mind isn't just in the brain as commonly understood. The mind is everywhere. Wherever you put your attention, there it is. There is a common misnomer regarding the synchronicities taking place in your life. Whenever you have an experience "out there" it is simply a direct reflection of what is occurring in your mind. Sometimes it seems rather mysterious and coincidental but nevertheless a natural occurrence.

Opening your mind to the presence of possibilities beyond normal understanding allows for their occurrence. Be willing to put forth the effort in training your mind to think even more is possible. Always allow room for greater understanding because there is always more to know and learn about the workings of your mind. A tremendous freedom comes to the mind willing to take chances and open itself to new experiences and greater understandings.

Communication between separate minds and separate bodies is difficult. Meaningful communication failed along with the belief in separation. Words alone never fully convey the messages being sent. The spoken word is often misunderstood. It is the feelings behind the words, which are received. If you spoke kind words to someone, but had anger and resentment towards the person, it is this feeling they would receive. We appear to be separate minds in separate bodies but the truth is we are one. We may have separate vehicles through which to express our separate ideas of ourselves, but our essence is shared. When you come to know wholeness, communication between all life forms, living or "dead" will be a natural outcome.

During a meditation one day, I connected with my husband and instantly saw a picture of him getting into his car. I was also aware of the feelings he was having at that moment. When I got up, I went to see what time it was and he would have been getting out of work at that time. When he got home I asked him if he were thinking what I had received and he said he had been. We are not separate from each other; we only seem to be.

Our mind is a powerful tool of communication as well. People ignore the potential of the mind because they do not believe in other possibilities. Telepathy for instance is a mode of communication readily available to those who are open to it. Reading minds is easy because we are all connected. We already experience each other telepathically, but many of us are not aware of it and discount it as something else.

The greatest obstacle to communication is judgment. When we judge another, we are separating ourselves from them, hence limiting communication. If you want to learn to experience telepathy, let go of judgment. I remember one day I was listening to the radio in the car and I didn't particularly care for the DJ because of the way he over-accented his words. He had a very nice voice but he was obviously trying too hard. All of a sudden I recognized the effects of my judgment. I realized I could listen to him without the negative opinion. I started to listen to what he was saying. Right before he began to describe someone, I automatically picked up the name of the person he was talking about. It was an unusual name and I normally would not have known it. The moment I stopped judgment, I readily received his thoughts. This often happens to me when I least expect it. The moment I concentrate on the process it evades me.

Whenever you are willing to see the manifestation of the amazing possibilities available to you, you will see their occurrence. Many people experience psychic abilities and express it as a gift from God. Some experience these gifts only in emergency situations. In reality, these are abilities we all share because they are simply qualities shared in the experience of a whole mind. However, we do have the power to determine whether or not we will use them.

We all have a whole mind; we simply see it as separate and create this reality. It doesn't change the fact we are whole just because we refuse to see it. The power of our mind takes any belief and creates a reality reflecting it. To see other realities and have other experiences ordained as extraordinary, is simply to open up to other possibilities.

Some people claim to speak to those whom have passed over. It is often discounted as crazy and impossible, and so for those it is. In actuality it is normal and natural to experience other realms. Mind does not need time or space. The physical and non-physical worlds are both attainable through thought. It is only the idea of time and space, which creates the impossibility in some minds. It is a blessing to know there is no death and we are eternal. To open yourself up to communication with those who have left the physical plane, simply accept it as a possibility. Intend to have the experience and let go of any fear that may discourage you from it.

Life is so exciting when we become aware of our wholeness and our connection with all of life. There is so much more to experience in this life. People often seek for excitement externally because life has become boring. Life is a treasure and we need to recognize we hold the keys to discovering it. So often we spend our lives trying to fill the emptiness we feel because of our sense of separateness. We are divine creations and seeking to rediscover our wholeness is an adventure and a journey worth taking. The rewards are infinite and will always be with us. The true rewards in life become a part of us and can never be taken away.

As for now, become a part of life by choosing to see everything as a part of you. Even the precious animals upon your plane are one with you. It is very possible to communicate with them once you remove the shades from your eyes. You do not need words to communicate. Animals readily practice the art of telepathy. They also know things before they happen. You have managed to bury your extrasensory perceptions but your animals rely on them. Your dog or cat is more than you think they are. Like everything else in life, animals are whatever your thought projections indicate. You see them the way you think about them. Whatever you decide to color them with in your mind is what they become to you.

In order to understand the workings of the human mind you need only perceive the unity of all of life. Then it becomes easy to understand the possibilities of telepathy, psychic abilities and other "extrasensory perceptions." In actuality they are not unusual phenomenon but rather natural occurrences. We have hindered our internal senses by relying on external data to determine our feelings. Extra sensory perceptions are not really extra at all. If we relied on internal cues rather then external, we would always know what steps to take at any given time. Only separate minds would find these practices difficult at best. With this understanding in mind, ponder the implications of the reality you are living and how you can indeed change the world.

Perhaps it is time to discover the power inherent "within" each of us. The infinite power of your mind is acknowledged as you let go of ideas and concepts you hold that are limiting and destructive to the creation of the life you want to live. Imagine the life you would like to live and let go of thoughts that tell you it is impossible to live it. The only difference between the person living the life of their dreams and one who isn't, is the belief in its possibility. The person living the life of their dreams is not willing to allow doubt to control the outcome. They imagine their dream and fully intend to achieve it. *"There is no limit to the power of a Son of God, but he can limit the expression of his power as much as he chooses. Your mind and mine can unite in shining your ego away; releasing the strength of God into everything you think and do."* (ACIM, I. p.64, 8;2,3)

Sometimes we think that living the life of our dreams will create the happiness we feel we are missing in our life. The power to create any life we desire is a part of who we are but happiness is a choice we make each moment. Happiness is a state of mind that results from acknowledging our divinity. Happiness is a state of being and is not dependent on external arrangements. Happiness that is dependent on something outside of us requires a constant arrangement in order to continue to experience it. For example, if I think money makes me happy, I will be busy striving to achieve more and more of it. There will never be enough and I will never be truly happy.

True happiness is a choice you make each moment and comes when you live in the present. The present moment is where true happiness resides. Giving thanks for everyone and everything presently in your life is where you will find serenity. Focusing on what is not in your life simply creates more lack.

What are you thinking? You experience exactly what you are thinking about. You are free to change it at will if you are not happy with your experience. Simply, you are what you think at any given moment. Go one step beyond thought and you will find serenity. When you choose to rise above thought, you know you are more than simply reacting to the thoughts you think. You are the thinker, as well as the spaces in between the thought where there is quiet and peace. For a moment visualize a bubbling brook, hearing the sounds of water gently spiraling down the rocks below. Just the thought of this can still the busy mind and bring forth a rush of peace. Contemplate peace and you are there.

Some people choose to be at the mercy of the thoughts and beliefs they hold. "It's just the way I am," they say, rather than "it is just the way I choose to be." We hold patterns in our minds of the way we are and never think of going beyond it. If there are any changes we want to make in our life we simply have to know it is possible. All we have to do is change our mind. For instance, with addiction, the focus is put on a substance as a source of fulfillment. The mind continues to repeatedly seek out the substance and the person feels driven by the substance. They think they are out of control when in reality they are only being driven by what they have instructed their mind to do.

I remember when I would find myself driving to the liquor store when I really knew it wasn't the answer for me. I felt completely at the mercy of thoughts seeking out alcohol. It wasn't until I felt empowered to make changes in my thoughts and my life that I was able to overcome the desire. I was able to realize that thoughts didn't happen to me and I had the power to change them. I am not at the mercy of my thoughts. In order to be absolutely at peace and free from substance abuse I had to make the connection in my mind and understand the power I truly had available to me.

I was in an AA program for about four months. I disagreed with their philosophy on powerlessness and I knew that there had to be a way to achieve complete freedom from addiction. It served its purpose for me in a short time and I overcame the "disease" of alcoholism. I have been cured at the level where the addiction was created, and that is in my mind. After all, isn't everything created from the mind? If not, then where does it begin? Are we at the mercy of influences that determine our destiny? If we believe this to be true, then sure enough our lives will unfold in a carefully orchestrated manner which supports this belief.

Somehow people feel a sense of connection and belonging when they share an illness. Why not share wholeness, for it is something that belongs to all of us? If I were to write a program of recovery it would include freedom rather than bondage and power rather than powerlessness. I would certainly not begin a meeting with the words,

"Hi, I am Mary and I am an alcoholic." I AM, are two very powerful words and they can be used in a powerful manner. Hi, I am Mary and I am willing to be free! This is just one example of changing the upside down thinking of support groups. We can get together and sob about how miserable we have made our lives or we can decide to change and create whatever changes are necessary. We can take back our power.

Whenever you face a difficulty in your life, choose to see the solution rather than the problem. If you put your attention on the problem, you simply become more aware of the problem. Putting your attention on the solution changes the outcome to a more positive favor. Whatever you focus on in your life will increase as well. The power of your mind to create is incredible and you need to guard your thoughts carefully. Your thoughts are the seeds of creation. If you focus on being an alcoholic, then your experience will support this attention. If you focus on freedom from addiction, your experience will reflect this attention. Where you choose to put your focus will determine the results.

The mind is not limited to the body. If a person's beliefs suggest their mind is limited to the body than that will be their experience. People have had out of body experiences where their awareness is outside of their body. Your awareness can leave the body. It does every night when you go to sleep. A part of your mind recognizes itself in a body but there is more to you than this. One day when I was meditating, I fell asleep. The next thing I knew I woke up before my body actually woke up. In other words, I had conscious awareness outside of my body. It is difficult to explain but nevertheless quite an extraordinary experience.

Edgar Cayce used to read books while he was sleeping. He was recognized as the sleeping prophet. Of course your mind is active while you sleep or your body would die. We may not be aware of it but we accomplish a great deal while our body sleeps. Discovering your true nature can be an exciting venture if you are willing to open yourself to other possibilities.

A COURSE IN MIRACLES discusses the illusion of the body and

I think it is very important to reiterate some of it in relation to addiction. The body is the ego's creation and so in order to understand the body in relation to the addiction process it is important to understand that it is not real. This is truly difficult to fathom because we see and experience it. In order to relieve some of your disbelief it may be easier to understand that the meaning you have assigned to the body is not real.

The ego created sickness, pain, misery and even death. You are not your body. Identifying yourself as your body is what creates all the sickness in the world. *"Sickness and perfection are irreconcilable. If God created you perfect, you are perfect. If you believe you can be sick, you have placed other gods before Him." (ACIM, I. p.187,1;3-5).* We were created perfect, whole and complete and any interpretations less than this, are created by the ego to ensure its existence. I have had many experiences that have taught me the meaning I had assigned to my body was not the meaning God intended for me. Whenever I was shown spiritual vision, it did not include my body.

My mind has wavered many times between ego and Spiritual vision. It has taken some time for me to integrate my experiences and let go of the rule the ego has taken in my own mind. As I vacillate back and forth between states of wholeness and feelings of separateness, I can clearly see the experience that each brings forth. There is tremendous power behind the thought and when the foundation is based on separation, it is easy to see the effect that results. *"Freedom must be impossible as long as you perceive a body as yourself. The body is a limit. Who would seek for freedom in a body looks for it where it cannot be found. The mind can be made free when it no longer sees itself as in a body, firmly tied to it and sheltered by its presence. If this were the truth, the mind were vulnerable indeed!" (ACIM, II. p.382, 1; 1-5)*

When we see ourselves as our body, our state of mind becomes dependent on how we control the way the body feels. We think the body controls how we feel, so we search relentlessly for ways to alter our feelings through external means. We seek external stimulation in the form of addictions. Disease itself is a manifestation of our belief the body is in control rather than the mind. We become a victim of our own bodies, as our beliefs dictate.

If you ever watch the Discovery channel and you see tribes in Africa practicing ancient methods of healing or voodoo and you think it is ridiculous; think again. There is power in belief regardless of the method used and our methods of healing are not any different. They may be more convincing to the mind but nevertheless, healing is the result. Of course healing is only temporary to the mind perceived as separate from God. True healing is the acknowledgment of our perfect union with God.

Addiction is the striving for a state of mind achieved through the body. Once you recognize it is the mind that has the power, the body loses significance and addictive feelings disappear. Our addictive feelings are only the result of the thoughts we are thinking. Our bodies simply respond to our thoughts. You can change your thoughts.

Remember, a craving is simply a bodily response to a thought. Change the thought and you will change the response.

It isn't about what you are doing that creates change in your life. It is about what you are, and if you choose to experience it or not. If you are feeling that there is too much work to be done in order to experience peace and freedom from addiction, then you will be happy to know there is nothing that you need to do. It isn't about what your body does. It is about releasing your mind. Of course, learning to quiet your mind and listen to the still small voice takes persistence and attention.

You are not alone and will soon learn you never have been; you only seemed to be. When you isolate yourself and put your attention on the things the body does, you feel separate and alone. When you switch your focus to the mind and experience wholeness once again, life becomes a joy ride.

Mind, Body and Spirit are one. If you see yourself as a body, your world is focused around supplying its needs. If you see yourself as a mind in a brain, then intellectual stimulation is always necessary. If you see yourself as Spirit, you somehow manage to separate yourself from it never really knowing what it is. If you know you are Mind, Body and Spirit as one, your viewpoint changes dramatically and you recognize wholeness. Many people find this hard to believe and of course it is, until you experience it otherwise. You simply have to be willing to see things differently.

You have the power to overcome any of the illusions you have created in your life. It doesn't matter what the addiction may be, you have the power to overcome it. If you place your faith in weakness, you know the outcome. When you place your faith in God, you may not know the outcome but it will assuredly be the most miraculous.

Death

When the physical body can no longer be used as a vehicle, due to lack of health or deterioration, a person leaves their body. As with everything in life I believe it is a matter of choice. What determines the rate at which the body deteriorates? I believe it is the person's thoughts, beliefs and ideas about it that create it. The mind is powerful and whatever your ideas about aging, disease and death may be, it will agree with you. Most of us agree with the ideas of genetics and tend to age along the same rate as our parents.

Years ago things were different. People aged quicker and had difficulty with their physical bodies much earlier in life. Today, there are ninety-year-old people who enjoy a healthy physical life. They refuse to believe in getting old the old-fashioned way. It is wonderful when a few break away from the constraints and dictates of society and choose their own way.

I remember when my grandpa had heart complications and he was instructed not to play golf or do a lot of physical work. Exercise wasn't recommended because it was feared to create more problems. My grandpa loved cleaning the garage and keeping himself busy. Little was taken into account between the body and the mind. My grandpa's body deteriorated even further when he couldn't enjoy doing the things he loved. Now they recommend physical exercise even with heart transplants. It is also detrimental to a person's health when they stop doing what they love.

They are always changing what is and is not good for us. I suppose this is because our beliefs and attitudes about things are constantly changing. I remember when I used to believe everything I heard as far as research and studies about the effects of certain foods on our bodies. It really all depends on who is doing the study and what it is they want to prove.

A COURSE IN MIRACLES talks a lot about cause and effect. *"If I intervened between your thoughts and their results, I would be tampering with a basic law of cause and effect; the most fundamental law there is. I would hardly help you if I depreciated the power of your own thinking." (ACIM, I. p.31.1;4-6s)* The power of our thoughts is a gift and we create through thought. Could it be that we create effects through our thoughts and then link the cause with something else such as an idea, substance or procedure? We have a headache and we think the cause is out there so we pop pills. Could it be the cause is our thoughts and the effect is the headache? We take a pain reliever and note in our mind that our headache will soon disappear and so it does. Which came first, the chicken or the egg as they say? Is it the pain reliever or the belief behind the thought, which cures?

Pay close attention to your thoughts. It is interesting to note the creative effects of our thoughts. We create thoughts backed by the beliefs we hold. If we hold a limiting belief that allows us to think in terms of lack and limitation, then a reevaluation is necessary to achieve freedom from it. If I believe I only live from paycheck to paycheck, then my thinking life and expectations will follow along these lines. If you don't know how to change limiting beliefs, I suggest monitoring your thoughts so you can discover what your beliefs actually are. It is possible to change them once you acknowledge the beliefs that seem to have a hold on you. Practice changing your thoughts and let go of expectations based on previous experience. If you expect the future to flow from the past, you simply bring it with you.

As we explore our minds and the potential each of us carries with us, we recognize the power beneath the surface of our limited self and we become free to explore other possibilities. Once we let go of limiting thoughts and beliefs about ourselves, we loosen the chains and freedom is acknowledged. We begin down the road of wholeness and our thoughts and feelings about our life are easily seen reflected in our surroundings.

I had a dream that I was flying and I was without my physical body. I was flying effortlessly down a road surrounded by trees on both sides. I remember contemplating which direction I was headed. I was aware of a powerful presence around me that seemed to be in charge of the whole show. In other words, my conscious self was being guided and I knew this as I pondered where I was headed. There was a tremendous freedom from ordinary fears. I could choose where I wanted to go and I trusted this presence to guide me there. This presence was a part of me and it was a strong and powerful force that I could sense was in charge. It may not have been an ordinary dream but it certainly revealed a lot to me. The power is with us and we need to trust it to guide our journey through life.

What if this powerful force is always with us and we never have anything to worry about? What if we spend our moments in worry and fear because we have failed to rely on our higher self for guidance and direction? It seems we have put our faith in outside sources for safety and have relied on physical senses to guide our way through life. I know I have had countless experiences where a powerful presence has come to my aid. Our Spirit is a powerful presence that is always with us and can keep us safe if we trust in it. Of course, our faith is always rewarded no matter what form it takes.

I suppose if you lack faith to begin with, then you have to ask for help in protection. Knowing you are always safe and that your Spirit will keep you safe requires an intense desire to know thyself. Coming to know you is a process that requires careful consideration. If you always put God outside of your own being, then you separate yourself from each other and from life. You may feel like you are a separate being who is having an isolated experience. You think you are prey to outside forces which control your destiny. What if this is only true if you make it true?

Acknowledging our divinity has fallen by the wayside. We continue relentlessly to worship other beings that have realized self. Why not understand and learn from their example rather than worship them as if it is unattainable for us? The bible was written with the intention of conveying messages that can be useful in our own life. However, it is often interpreted from an ego state and has been used to spread fear rather than love. *"The bible is a fearful thing in the ego's judgment. Perceiving it as frightening, it interprets it fearfully". (ACIM, I. P.87, 4; 5, 6) A COURSE IN MIRACLES* describes several examples of how the ego's interpretations are misleading. *"I will visit the sins of the fathers unto the third and fourth generation," as interpreted by the ego, is particularly vicious. It becomes merely an attempt to guarantee the ego's own survival. To the Holy Spirit, the statement means that in later generations He can still reinterpret what former generations had misunderstood, and thus release the thoughts from the ability to produce fear." (ACIM, I. P.87, 8;1-3)*

I have consciously meditated with the idea in mind of connecting with Jesus and learning from his life. Each time I feel a presence convey the message of looking to self and finding the love that is there. The focus is put back on me as if to say "the answers are a part of you as well." If I worship Jesus, I am putting him on a pedestal and separating myself from him. I can only recognize the love in him, when I recognize it in myself.

Christ consciousness is a part of all of us. It is the unity that exists between minds that perceive themselves as separate because their attention is on their bodies. In this world the focus is put on our bodies and this reinforces the belief in separation. If just for a moment, you connect with the part of your self that is one with all of life, you will open a door into a new world. In the truest sense, we are separate in the sense of our abilities to express ourselves, but our constitution is the same. The essence of our minds is consciousness and its expression is the Christ. In order to understand the enormity of consciousness, one need only recognize its presence everywhere. There isn't anywhere that we are not.

We think of creation as having a beginning and an ending. It is difficult to imagine life without it, but it is possible. Does thought have a beginning and an ending? Is there a time when creation stands still? I think not. In order to open our minds to other possibilities we need to challenge the beliefs and limitations we currently hold. Beliefs and thoughts passed down from generation to generation are not necessarily true because they last. Beliefs are powerful and form the framework for a person's life. Why live our lives in chains when we hold the keys to freedom? The kingdom of heaven is waiting to be discovered. It is and always has been a part of you.

Some religions speak of sin and claim retribution if there isn't some sort of atonement for them. I do not believe this myself. People condemn themselves. It would be pointless for God to do it. Apparently we were given free will and I don't think it means only in certain conditions. If we commit any act against another living being, we pay for it immediately. The emotions are recorded in our soul. Anger itself is punitive. We direct anger at others but nevertheless it is destructive to ourselves. In order to experience the emotion of anger we have to believe we are victims to begin with, placing blame outside of ourselves. It is the whole thought system that needs restructuring in order to be free of hostility, anger and hatred.

Look at an individual who is prejudiced against certain races or religions. Often times, they blame everything on a particular race for the problems in their life. A person that extends hatred to another person cannot separate themselves from the hate. They become hatred, so inevitably they destroy themselves. If you blame another person for the conditions in your life, then you will never be able to change your circumstances. It is truly ignorant to hate another person or being at all for that matter. When you do this, you are separating yourself from them. It is no wonder a person with this belief system gets angry. How can a person change his or her life if someone else is at fault?

People who abuse animals and children certainly do not have to wait until death for punishment. Their minds punish them every day.

They hate themselves and project it outward. They somehow feel good about another person's detriment. They do not feel love in themselves or they wouldn't be able to withhold love from another.

In all simplicity, our thoughts create. Do you create from fear or love? The choice is yours to make each moment. I am learning to monitor the thoughts I allow myself to think. I realize how quickly I can change my thoughts from fear to love. Anytime I find myself getting angry, I take note of my thoughts. I can change them immediately as soon as I recognize I do not want the consequences of the ones I have chosen.

We have become accustomed to thinking from a standpoint of fear. The limited self we have identified with over eons of existence cannot think with love. The existence of the ego or limited self is based on fear and separation. In order to be free from the constraints of the ego, it requires intense discipline. It has taken a long time to train our minds to react to external events as if they are separate from us.

We choose how we react to external cues. If we live life as if our behavior is controlled from "out there," then someone else is always at the controls and we are at their mercy. It is as if we have become like robots, pre-programmed to react to life. Our minds simply react to events or persons, as if there is no other way. They say insanity is doing the same thing over and over again, expecting a different result. I think that would qualify us for insanity. After all, we live our lives from day to day, without questioning the effects of our own thoughts. Someone else is responsible for our misfortunes. Again, it is all a part of denying our divinity. We are creators with a power beyond our wildest imaginations.

There are men and women who believe that power is to be attained from outside in, as well. Controlling other people and having power over them through the use of fear is considered powerful. To have a lot of money is recognized as being powerful because they are able to control a lot of situations or people. None of these are about power at all, but weakness. Only the weak need to control other people through the use of fear or force.

True power comes from within and is not about control at all. True power is a state of being, complete and whole with strength so strong, it isn't even necessary. Weakness and strength are ego terms because they are polarities describing a physical state of being. A better term to use when describing the strength of our whole self is absolute. There is no in-between here. Our whole self doesn't feel the need to control other people. It actually has no needs at all. Our whole self extends and expresses from a state of being that is whole and complete. Love is omnipresent and doesn't recognize fear or lack at all.

You can place your faith in an addiction and the power it holds over you or you can place your faith in God. To be destined to a life of addiction without any chance of real recovery, doesn't say much about God. Place your faith where you will see the best results. You do not have to be a recovering alcoholic or addict all of your life. Only when the ego is in charge would you be destined to this life. When God is in charge, all things are possible. Good luck on your journey of discovery. I know it will be an exciting venture for you to come to know your true self.

Abundance

A COURSE IN MIRACLES describes depression as a state of mind that feels deprived of something it wants. It says we are only deprived because of a choice we have made in our minds and we simply need to choose otherwise. When we observe the thoughts we allow ourselves to think, we can discard a lot of the limiting beliefs that have created a sense of lack and limitation. Nothing happens to us. If we have created lack and limitation in our life, we can choose otherwise.

I know it is difficult for some people to believe in the power of their own mind. They have convinced themselves they are powerless and are at the mercy of outside influences, including God. As long as you allow yourself to think along these lines, freedom will evade you. You will indeed be at the mercy of a force outside you, because that will be where you have placed your faith. Coming to a realization that we are perfect, whole and complete, involves letting go of all the ideas and beliefs that are in the way of this recognition.

I remember a time when my husband and I lived on a relatively low income. I constantly worried about paying the bills. Our paychecks would come in and we would pay the bills with very little left for leisure. One day, I recognized the bills always got paid and I needed to stop worrying about it. I had a strong belief in paying our debts and not paying the bills was just not a part of my script.

At the time, the beliefs I held in my mind were sufficient to feel lack even if I had a million dollars. It wouldn't have been enough money for the lack I felt within my own being. Of course, now I can look back at my life and know I created every detail. When we wanted to have children, we knew we wanted to have a home of our own first. We didn't want to have a family in a rented apartment. Eventually, we were able to purchase a home and have the family we desired. Many people have families and live in unpleasant conditions but we were not willing to have a family until we were prepared. Hence, we had the motivation to create this in our lives.

Abundance is achieved through a state of mind that doesn't recognize lack. You simply know money is energy and will continue to flow in your life as long as you do not impede it with your thoughts. Many times I have heard reference to the ebb and flow, meaning there are times when more money is coming in then going out and visa versa. If it has any meaning at all it would have to pertain to the thoughts you allow yourself to entertain in your mind. If you spend a bit more money on a given day than you wish you would have, there is a tendency for fear to enter your mind. The ebb would then come into play because you have a corresponding thought linked with fear. Otherwise we are at the mercy of something outside of our own beings.

Many times I have heard comments regarding the inflow of money at a time in a person's life when they needed it most. They also had faith in allowing income to come from other sources. How often have you had extra money come unexpectedly from out of nowhere? An unexpected refund suddenly comes across your path. Watch your thoughts and beliefs about money to determine how to change what isn't working for you. You have had the power to create lack and limitation and you have the same potential to create wealth.

Creation is a part of who you are. You can have anything in this world you choose to have as long as you let go of thoughts and beliefs that stand in the way. Money and things do not create peace or happiness but are simply things that make it more comfortable or pleasurable. As a divine expression of life you are entitled to whatever your heart desires. Creating is simply an ability which is all a part of who you are. When money or things are sought above the recognition of Spirit, a person becomes sidetracked. There isn't anything outside of our own being that will bring us lasting peace and happiness.

Of course, the appropriate actions are necessary to create the abundance you deserve. However, you will only ask for the salary you feel entitled to, which will be based on the value you attach to yourself and your abilities. Open yourself up to increasing the value you have placed upon yourself in whatever means necessary. Remember, you only get what you ask for and oftentimes you will sell yourself short. When you come to know yourself you will also recognize there is no limit to your worth.

It is all too easy to lose your self in this world. The most important thing you can ever do for yourself and others is to know yourself as God created you. Coming to know the love you are and express this love is the greatest accomplishment you can make in this life. There is nothing in this life that you can physically achieve that will ever surpass what you can accomplish through a state of being that has realized the energy of love.

I suppose some people believe that having a lot of money would allow them to live a life free from the constraints of fear. Perhaps certain fears would be alleviated but they would most certainly be replaced with more appropriate fears. If a person believes money is the answer, of course they will fruitlessly search for salvation in the wrong place. The search for peace and happiness begins and ends with the discovery of your own spirit. Of course it is nice to have money but it is only an addition to life when fulfillment is already recognized.

A person never has enough money if it is where they seek for peace and freedom. There will always be more they have to accumulate. Placing freedom externally must therefore result in a continuous search for future fulfillment. Since peace and freedom are omnipresent, they cannot be found in a future state of being. The present moment is the only place peace can be recognized and it is never based on altered events or situations.

Recognizing creation as an extension of the abilities one has as a divine being enables one to allow, rather then feel a need to manifest. If you feel a need to manifest, you must first have a sense of lack. You feel a need to manifest when you have doubts in your mind about the potential for anything to appear in your life. When you know you will always have enough of something, you will always find it plentiful. In the truest sense, you do not lack anything; you simply haven't realized it yet. You do not lack anything in your life unless you have chosen to be denied. If you know your desires and experience them in your mind in the present moment as if they have been fulfilled, you will see them in your experience. Your beliefs may require challenging in these areas in order to open and expand your ability to receive from the infinite resources that are available.

Our desires are the groundwork of creation. Until we have a desire for something, it cannot be achieved or attained. If we cannot see it in our mind's eye, then we deny the possibility of its occurrence. If we feel something is impossible, then of course it will be. As I look back at my life, there isn't anything I truly desired that I haven't received. Of course I had to have faith linked with my desires or they couldn't have been attained.

The key to accomplishing anything in this life is desire. Right now my strongest desire is to know myself as God created me. I strongly know I am letting go of any interference to this realization. There isn't anything in this world that has greater value than recognizing our unity with all of life. It is something we take with us no matter where we go; in this life or the next expression.

A COURSE IN MIRACLES suggests that we do not value what is valueless and it has guidelines to follow concerning discernment into what actually has real value. *"First, if you choose a thing that will not last forever, what you chose is valueless". (ACIM, II. p.245,6;1) "Next, if you choose to take a thing away from someone else, you will have nothing left". (ACIM, II. p.246, 7;1)* A person who steals from someone else in order to have something he perceives he cannot have otherwise, is only reinforcing the lack he feels within. His thoughts surround the belief in lack and he will only create more of it.

This brings me to the lessons concerning giving and receiving. ACIM says giving and receiving are one in truth. To give is to receive. Whenever we give something to another, are we not doing it for ourselves? It may seem as if we are giving to another for unambiguous reasons, but are we not getting something in return? Certainly we get a good feeling out of giving to another person. We may receive feelings associated with being a rescuer or hero. We may receive gratitude we feel placated to receive. Do we not get upset when someone doesn't appreciate our gifts or fails to give appropriate gratitude? If someone doesn't say, "thank you," do you somehow feel cheated? We expect gratitude when we give to another, is this not true? And if we do, aren't we expecting something in return? We are giving to receive.

Of course, there are those who give out of the kindness of their own hearts. They are able to give without expectation, acknowledgement or reward. They inherently understand that to give is to receive and it is a basic universal law. Whenever we give of ourselves to others, do we not trust that the same shall be done for us? If I give financial assistance to someone in need without personal acknowledgment, am I truly giving? If to give is to receive then perhaps I am.

I know without a doubt that if I give to someone, I will not have less, but more. If I were to give thinking that I lose, then of course I will tend not to give. However, if I have the knowledge that giving is receiving then I will reverse my thinking from lack to abundance. As I share, I receive. If I take something away from someone because I want it for myself, the feelings I get are those of lack. I feel lack within if I feel I need to take something from someone else in order to receive. In return I simply create more lack.

I understand that when I give monetarily to someone who has doubts about their financial situation, I am assisting them temporarily unless I teach them to change their minds about it. The difference between the person on the street and someone who has a home is their thoughts and beliefs about their life. Our beliefs form the foundation for the possibility for anything to manifest in our lives.

We are one, and to give is to receive. The greatest gift anyone can give to another is his or her acknowledgment of unity. When we come to know ourselves as love, we can truly give it, simply by being and extending the love we are. As we acknowledge feelings of wholeness, we are able to share them with each other. There is no greater gift than the expression of love. It is the only gift that has value.

We can only give what we have received. Someone who feels separate and isolated with feelings of contempt for life will most likely give from a standpoint of fear. Someone who knows who they are and feels fulfilled from within will certainly give of himself or herself with love.

We treat other people in accordance with the way we feel about ourselves. If someone is abusive or neglectful of animals or children, just imagine what they are feeling inside. They are filled with hatred and fear and simply project it outside of themselves. Oftentimes when we hear stories of abuse, we attack the abuser. Certainly the abuser needs prayers of love and forgiveness. If we give attack and hatred to someone who experiences attack and hatred, are we not like them? Giving and receiving are indeed one at a level of wholeness. In a world of separation, certainly they appear different.

The most important gift we can give to the world is to know ourselves as one with God. Jesus certainly had a lot to give and they were not material gifts, but gifts of the heart.

Of course, a lot of what Jesus taught has been misinterpreted from a standpoint of fear. Nevertheless, the truth is available to those who truly desire to be free from the constraints of the world. Remember, we see what we choose to see. If we desire to continue to see the world through the eyes of fear and limitation, then that is what we will see.

The very basics of giving and receiving have to do with the very thoughts we allow ourselves to think about others and ourselves. What we think about others, directly effects how we feel. When we give thoughts of love and acceptance, we receive love and acceptance. When we give thoughts of attack and condemnation, we feel attacked and condemned. Very basic to the laws of cause and effect are those of giving and receiving. Everyone is potentially our personal savior depending on how we choose to see them. It is essential to the human race that these principles are understood because then we would stop mis-creating and learn to live at peace with each other and ourselves.

We receive what seem to be the gifts we offer to others. When it comes to unity it is easily recognized that giving and receiving go hand in hand. When we send thoughts of love and acceptance to another person we are receiving the feelings from those thoughts. A person may express feelings characteristic to those of hatred and bigotry. If we judge and condemn them for it, then we have experienced the effects of those judgments. If someone is acting from a standpoint of fear and hatred, they are truly seeking love. Love is what will assist them in going beyond their current ability to express themselves without fear.

True abundance from the infinite resources available to us through universal energy is omnipresent. Lack is not a term that can be used to describe varying degrees of receiving it because it *is*. We either allow ourselves to receive from the infinite universe or we do not. There are no opposites in the mind of God. Opposites are terms the ego uses. Be open to receiving the eternal gifts available to each of us. Eternal gifts stay with us because they are a part of who we are.

It is the identification with our egos that has separated us from truth. When we separate ourselves from each other and God we separate ourselves from the acknowledgment of wholeness. In turn we feel deprived and our lives reflect this feeling. *"A sense of separation from God is the only lack you really need correct". (ACIM, I. p.14,2;1)* The greatest feelings come from an awareness of wholeness and unity. Along with this recognition is the knowledge that there isn't anything we are deprived of without our permission.

We are co-creators with God. Like God, we were given the same abilities to create through the power of our own minds. Our thoughts are the seeds of manifestation. Our beliefs nurture and allow them to grow. Our own thoughts can impede as well as encourage our God-given creative potential. We impede the progress of our goals with negative expectations and resistance. The appropriate actions necessary to take in order to accomplish anything will reveal themselves. We simply acknowledge our desires and then let them go. If we try to control the outcome, we create resistance and we simply block the desired occurrence. We create an energy surrounding the conditions of the creation of our goal that is counterproductive.

One day I came across a list of things that I desired to create in my life. I had forgotten that I had written them down but I had a strong desire to have the items on the list. Nevertheless, by the time I found the list, I already received the items listed. I received everything to the last detail. It is important to be careful about what you ask for because you usually get it. You will often ask for less than you are entitled to because you think it is impossible or you lack self-worth. There are many different reasons to limit yourself and your life. You need only monitor your thoughts to discover what those limitations are for you.

You create from a present state of being. You simply acknowledge your desires, know they will occur, and allow them to happen. You feel them in your mind as if they have already occurred. You feel them in your present state of mind. In other words you do not feel lack in the present and pray it is filled through changes in the external world. You will reinforce the feelings of lack if that is where you place your focus. Do you trust your dream or goal will be accomplished or do you know it? Knowingness is absolute and is the key to creation.

It is fun to acknowledge the power of our minds to create the life of our dreams. The only limitation is the one we create in our minds. Remember the external and internal worlds are really the same. Be open and receptive to expanding the perimeters of your mind. You will discover the only perimeters are those that are self-imposed. It is certainly a thrill to discover our creative potential is truly unlimited.

In conclusion, I would have to say that you do not lack anything in your life except by choice. You may not recognize it but you have made a decision in your mind that tells you something is impossible to achieve or obtain. Lack implies that a future state of being is where you will find peace. Truthfully, peace is in the present moment and cannot be acknowledged as long as you are projecting salvation in a future state of being. If you are living in a condition of poverty, you need only acknowledge it is your creation and step beyond it. Change your mind about what it is you would like to experience in life and allow it to occur. If you change your mind, you will change your experience.

Beliefs and Fear

How do we get beyond the belief systems we hold which limit and distort our view of the world? I believe it all begins with intention. We intend to understand ourselves more clearly and we have to be willing to let go of anything inauthentic. Understanding ourselves is a process of letting go of ideas and definitions we currently hold. You have to let go of everything you think love is, in order to make room for truth. I have only seen a glimpse of the totality of the essence of love. It is truly amazing when we open ourselves up to discovering this immense force within us.

By understanding that truth *is*, we begin to see that the world is simply a reflection of our beliefs. Beliefs really limit and judge by attempting to define and explain the unexplainable. For instance, I do not claim a particular religious denomination simply because I refuse to define and limit God. For me, life is all about knowing God. God is everywhere.

The mind has the power to create from doubt or faith. "Without a doubt," implies perfect faith. Do you know what would happen if you had perfect faith every moment of your existence? You would know peace. Take any event and imagine the outcome with faith. Take the same event and imagine it with doubt. The only difference between faith and doubt is in one instance you expect a positive outcome and the other one you do not.

If you want to recognize the outer world as simply a reflection of the inner world, take note of what is on your mind. When you buy a new car, all of a sudden you see more cars just like the one you bought. Were they always there before and you just didn't notice them? Whatever you focus on in your mind is what you see outside. In reality, the outer and inner world is the same, but in order to understand this you need to pay attention to the workings of your mind.

Whenever you contemplate an idea and superimpose your thoughts onto the canvas of life, you create. Why do you create from a space of fear and lack? You allow yourself to hold ideas and beliefs about yourself that create it. In order to create a life from a space of perfect peace and knowingness, you have to transcend your normal way of thinking. How do you do this? You simply have to be willing to see things differently and then you will be shown the way.

You can transcend the world of fear you have created. Whenever you are in fear, you are not recognizing your higher self. You are identifying with the ego and limiting your own vision. I know if you let go of the need to control the outcome of events, you lesson fear. It is not the responsibility of your limited self to take care of you. Knowing there is a perfect order in life allows you to flow with it rather than resisting it. It is the resistance that creates fear and pain.

Transformation is a process that occurs in the mind. Salvation is all about changing your mind about who you think you are. Believing you are separate from one another and from God simply reinforces the limiting beliefs you hold. To reach beyond your present state of awareness requires intensive restructuring of your whole thought system. As of now, it originates from feelings of sin and guilt. The original sin is nothing more than your belief in separation because all of your mistakes stem from this single cause. You feel anger and hatred within and project it outside of yourself in an attempt to get rid of it. Unfortunately, you simply reinforce the feeling of separation, encouraging hatred and fear to grow.

We are perfect, whole and complete. It is only our beliefs about ourselves which prevent us from feeling whole within. Our world is torn asunder in an attempt to escape from the prison we have created in our minds. Indeed, a prison of the mind doesn't require bars to hold us captive. We attempt to escape this world we have created through a process called projection. We displace our internal thoughts and feelings outside of ourselves, thinking that is where they originate. We are stuck trying to control the world perceived to be outside of ourselves. In truth, nothing exists that isn't a part of you.

For eons we have allowed our minds to be controlled through fear. Fear is a tactic used by our ego that literally feeds it and keeps it alive. Without fear, where would we be? Paradise sounds like the perfect way to describe this state of being. Our minds would return to their original state of being where only the knowledge of wholeness exists. We can be in paradise here on earth. We have to challenge our minds to release fear and attack which reinforce the feelings of separation. In truth, we are perfect, whole and complete. We simply have to rediscover ourselves and allow our minds to show us the way.

The heavens open their arms to embrace you and the recognition of your perfect union with all of life. Simply be willing to discover the magic and wonder available to you. The power is with you and it has never left you. You simply closed your eyes to truth. You just need to re-awaken to a state of being that is omnipresent. Be willing to let go of the illusions about yourself you have created and allow the truth to be revealed.

You will effortlessly let go of addictive behaviors that support the illusions. All that is necessary is a willingness to unlearn everything you think is truth right now. It is a journey well worth undertaking. The gifts go with you into eternity. Enjoy each moment of your life. Salvation is not in the future. It is here and now. Peace, joy and happiness are with you in the present moment. Simply let go of everything in your life that keeps your mind chained to the past. Future expectations of peace and happiness also keep you from enjoying the gifts of the present.

The most important message I can leave you with in this moment is to be thankful for the gifts presently in your life. The gift of love is the only one worth receiving. If you can't use the gift without a body, it is useless. Give and receive gifts of the heart and be grateful. Gratitude is a feeling that expands the soul into greater depths of feeling. If you focus on gratitude for the love in your heart, it expands.

Remember, whatever you focus on will increase. Every thought centered on love increases your awareness of it.

It seems to me that love is the reason we are here. It has to be, since love is the only thing of value here on earth. Love is who we are and discovering it as a part of us, is a freeing feeling. We realize it isn't about seeking love outside of ourselves. It is about knowing the love we are and extending this love to all we meet.

Trust the process will be one of joy, and let go of fear and apprehension. It is truly a magical experience to know we are one with God and all of life. What is there to fear when we know we are at the center of the universe and are the creator of all of our experiences? Sure enough, if we look to the media and experiences that other people have created through fear, it often fills us with fear. What if this horrible experience happens to us as well? Many people fear recognizing that they have created negative experiences because they do not understand why they would do something to themselves. No one intentionally wants to be harmed in any way, but the truth is our thoughts create. If our minds are filled with fear, fear will be reflected in our world. The good news is that if we connect with peace and love that is what we experience.

So how do we cast away thoughts of fear? After all, we have lived our lives with fear as our foundation. We have to change our thoughts and beliefs that support it. How do we do this? By stilling our minds and connecting with the silence; we learn to listen to the voice that speaks from the standpoint of peace and love. Many refer to this voice as the still, small voice. It is only small because we have stomped it out with the ego's voice. It is the egos voice that speaks through fear. It is easily recognized because our whole self never brings fear to our mind.

Monitor your thoughts and feelings and you will know if your foundation is built upon love or fear. Spend moments each day where you will not let fear exist in your mind. See how long you can keep fear at bay. You will probably notice within minutes, fear has encompassed your mind. It would be better to tell yourself that for a period of say ten minutes, you will only think thoughts of love, knowingness and bliss. Soon you will see where you have placed your attention, and the outcome you experience will be moments of peace.

If we tell ourselves not to experience something, where is our attention? Our attention becomes focused on the very idea or thing we want to avoid. This is another reason dieting doesn't work and why people struggle with recovery when it comes to addictive behaviors. What does AA focus on? Alcoholism and the disease that is "incurable." What do they get? People who feel powerless and at the mercy of their thoughts and feelings surrounding their addictive behaviors.

The very idea of a support program that supports the addiction is disturbing to me. Why not have a support program that empowers people to make the necessary changes in their lives without being a victim? We are not victims and we do have the power to change any thought, belief or experience in our life that we do not want to have. If we focus on empowerment and freedom, what do we get? If we focus on helplessness and powerlessness, what do we get? As soon as you begin the process of carefully monitoring what you allow yourself to think, you will see the effects. First you have to let go of the belief that thoughts happen to you. You do not have the power to change your thoughts until you recognize it is you who creates them.

Your thoughts create your feelings. You are never at the mercy of your emotions. Moods do not happen to you; they are chosen. Do not say, "I am in a good mood today." It only means that when you are in a bad mood, it is also with you for a day. "I choose to be in a good mood right now," is more appropriate, because you are not at the mercy of your moods. Moods simply change with the thoughts you allow yourself to think. If you are experiencing a mood you would rather not be in, change your mind. It is that simple.

Suppose that for an instant you could feel yourself floating on a cloud with no thoughts of fear or worries that enter your mind. You are looking down on earth and can view the life you are living from a perspective that is clearly without fear. Is there anything you would do differently in your life if you didn't have fear? Fear is a trap that imprisons the mind into living a life unfulfilled. It prevents you from living the life of your dreams. Connect with the peace and love that is a part of you, so you can release this fear. Fear prevents you from knowing yourself. Fear is not real because it is based on seeing reality through a clouded lens.

There are so many reasons to let go of fear that I couldn't possibly cover them all. Fear prevents us from living fully and appreciating the blessings currently in our lives. The notion of separation is what creates fear and it can be alleviated with the acknowledgment of wholeness. Nevertheless, it certainly maintains itself diligently and close monitoring of our thoughts and beliefs is necessary to achieve complete release from fear.

There are times I awake from dreaming and fear pervades my thoughts. What is it that I could be dreaming that is causing fear? In truth, we are dreaming when we experience fear because it isn't any more real than while we are sleeping. Fear seems real, especially when we experience the effects. It isn't real because the cause is not. Separation is not real, even if we believe it is so. We are one with God, and believing otherwise doesn't change the truth. It may change our experience of truth but nevertheless truth remains. Apparently we think we can change what God created because we continue to live a life based on a fictitious Rembrandt of our true self.

I know it seems far-fetched to believe that God created you perfect, whole and complete. After all, for eons you have believed you were sinful, wretched creatures that must pay for your sins. This notion doesn't say a lot about God. What kind of God would or could create anything less than itself? I tell you one thing; it is man who created these ideas about God. These ideas and limitations surrounding God came about with the creation of the ego. The sense of separation that came into being became the foundation for the hatred and destruction that occurs in the world now.

Many people give God credit when good things happen in their life and naturally, God must be responsible when something goes wrong as well. Fear pervades consciousness and prevents the God force from releasing us from the constraints of the world. As I look back on my life, I can see the unreality of fear. In every circumstance where there was danger, I was always given the instructions or the power to overcome the situation. There has never been a time that fear was useful. Fear just kept my mind busy and what did it accomplish? If we just stop, take a deep breath and align with peace in any given circumstance where we find ourselves at the mercy of fear, we instantly change how we feel. What is there to worry about that isn't already taken care of, if seen through the light of knowingness and faith?

We subject ourselves needlessly in a process of worry and fear that creates a busy mind. Do any of our fears ever manifest? I would have to say absolutely; because wherever we put our faith will be our experience. If we have faith in a fearful outcome then certainly this will be our experience. Most of the fears in my life that I have experienced have always been backed by a belief in the power of God to take care of me. This has to be the reason nothing really bad has happened in my life. Anything that I would consider dreadful in my life was self-inflicted. I created the thoughts and beliefs that sought peace and fulfillment through a bottle.

A lot of the horrible things that happen to people when they drink never happened to me. I always asked to be taken care of when I was under the influence and this was my experience. When I went to AA and listened to the stories surrounding people's addictions, I also discovered exactly what a person's belief system entailed. Some people felt completely unworthy and would create one bad situation after another. It was easy to see people who felt victimized by their own mind. I heard someone claim, "I always have to drive a car when I drink." This is definitely not a good belief to hold about yourself and alcohol. The combination can be deadly and it can also leave you with numerous DWI's and other consequences. If you listen to anyone talk long enough, you will get an idea of what their general beliefs are about life.

Focus on your intention to be free of limitations and to know thyself. The part of yourself that knows you are one with God will guide the way. You were given the Holy Spirit to lead the way. Of course the

Holy Spirit is as much a part of you as the illusions you hold. It is simply a shift in awareness.

Life is incredible and the journey itself is so rewarding. Of course, there are days when you may not feel completely holy because you allow your ego to rule. The important thing to note is never put yourself down for slipping and experiencing ego emotions such as anger and fear. If you put your attention on the behaviors you are not proud of, you simply reinforce them and they continue to manifest themselves.

The world is a place where you have come to discover the power of love. When you recognize yourself as love, you let go of the illusions you hold about yourself as well.

You truly transform from an ugly duckling to a beautiful swan. Life is magical and right now God is a part of you. When you absolutely know this truth, what is there to fear? *"What is the lesson for today except another way of saying that to know your Self is the salvation of the world? To free the world from every kind of pain is but to change your mind about yourself. There is no world apart from your ideas because ideas leave not their source, and you maintain the world within your mind in thought." (ACIM, II. p.243,10;1-3).* Understanding this is essential to the realization of freedom. You are the creator of bondage or freedom.

So what keeps us chained to the past where we remain in bondage to thoughts or ideas of who we think we are? I know that it is our thoughts and beliefs about our life that we carry with us. What we choose to believe about ourselves determines the thoughts we choose to think. When I fear something in my past, it is my thoughts and feelings about it that I bring with me into the present moment. If we stay in the present moment in our minds we can let the past go. For instance, in the past whenever I saw people drink alcohol, memories of the miseries associated with it would return to the forefront of my mind. There were also times I wished I could drink like a normal person. However, I no longer think like an alcoholic and do not need to think like one just because I am reminded of it. Whenever I am around someone who is drinking alcohol, I use it as an opportunity to be grateful for my own freedom. Now I have absolutely no desire to drink alcohol; even as a normal person.

So when you encounter an experience in life that is usually associated with a fearful reaction, how do you choose peace instead? For example, my husband's job is on the line once again. This will be the third time in a very short span of three years. He is a computer software engineer and one company after another has gone belly up. Once again, we find ourselves amidst the stress of being without an income. I am a stay-at-home mother and have not yet returned to work. We are now confronted with an opportunity to react with fear and resistance or choose the security of the unknown. He could lose his job any day. Of course, each time before when he has lost a job, something better has come along.

There are several ways we could choose to experience our life when there appears to be a potential loss of our steady source of income. I know everything will work out because it always does. On the other hand, my logical mind wants to run screaming like hell. How could this possibly work out when we have expenses to be paid? Last night I was lying in bed and for some reason my mind started wandering. I thought of different scenarios in my mind and each one had a fearful outcome. They were not fearful reactions to actual events, but imaginary ones that I somehow allowed myself to entertain. I then realized that fear about events that I thought were possibly going to happen, were not any different than the imaginary ones. I had never made this connection in my mind before. You may or may not understand what I am trying to say but perhaps you have allowed your mind to wander, creating fearful outcomes to imaginary events. For instance, fear concerning the "what-ifs" about circumstances in your life.

Nevertheless, there comes a time when you realize that God is your source, and your regular income is only an avenue upon which to receive it. I am going to challenge my mind to remain at peace and expect the best possible outcome in this circumstance. I need to bring to the forefront of my mind everything that I have learned in my life and during the completion of this book. I will keep you posted as to the outcome so that when you face a difficulty in your life, it will help you as well.

We do have the power to step beyond fear and choose peace and happiness regardless of our circumstances. I know that since I have made the choice to be at peace about our financial circumstances, I have felt it. I simply had to stop my mind from wandering and experiencing fearful thoughts. We are always provided for as long as we accept the power behind knowingness and faith. If we know without a doubt that we are always provided for, what do we do? We open the window where the opportunities of miracles can be provided in our lives. Miracles are natural occurrences but they are often stomped out with doubt and fear. How can we make room for the miracles in our lives if we are trusting in fear?

Miracles are simply a manifestation of a mind joined with God, where lack is not recognized and only wholeness exists. Sometimes we place our faith in fear because it seems to be the natural outcome of certain circumstances. Fear is the result of the belief in separation and therefore it only seems real in the world of dreams. Miracles seem beyond belief and are quite extraordinary to those who perceive themselves separate from God and each other. Miracles are actually quite natural and if they are not occurring in your life you have limited yourself and your life.

How do we create limitations in our lives? We choose to hold ideas and beliefs about ourselves that create them. How do we rid ourselves of destructive behaviors and addictions? First of all, we see that we are choosing our behaviors through our thoughts and the way we view our world. We begin by observing our thoughts and paying attention to the thoughts that lead to the behavior. We have the power to change our thoughts and align them with higher ideals. Focus on what you want to achieve in your life, rather than what you don't want. You simply have to desire freedom more than you want bondage to a substance or behavior.

Remember you are bound to a substance or behavior because of the feelings you think it brings you. You are truly searching for peace and fulfillment and when you are looking in the wrong place, you know it. You know it because you can never get enough of the substance you are seeking. When it comes from within, there is nothing you need. It is a part of you and you will not seek it outside of you. I remember contemplating how much I wanted freedom from addiction. At the time I wasn't aware of how to be free but I knew there was a way. I knew there were people who had freedom and I knew it was possible for me as well. I remember seeing a hawk soaring in the sky and that became my symbol of freedom.

True freedom didn't come to me until I realized I wasn't at the mercy of a force outside of my own being. Alcoholism wasn't something that had to control me either. I chose to think like an alcoholic and I could choose to be free as well. The real connection came to me when I was going to Alcoholics Anonymous. I became aware of the thoughts and beliefs that caused a person to think the way they did and how it affected their reality. Some people actually believed they were alcoholics for life and had to continue going to meetings or they would drink again. This whole belief system stems from a feeling of helplessness and it only perpetuates the disease rather than healing it. I remember thinking, "if alcoholism is a disease, then it is curable like any other disease."

People are subject to the beliefs of other people concerning helplessness because they have not yet learned to think for themselves. This whole belief system is what makes people vulnerable and creates stagnation in their lives. How can we get beyond something and rise above it if it has control over us? Then we do not make room for the miracle. The temptations that we place in power in our lives only have the power because we give it to them. *A Course in Miracles* explains that a temptation is simply a prayer that does not allow the miracle to touch some dreams. We call it a temptation and what does it become? If we are not so focused on the temptation fulfilling emptiness or giving us a feeling we don't think we have anyhow, it loses its value. Remember whatever we think about expands.

We get whatever we put our attention on. That is simply a power we inherently own as an extension of God. Our thoughts create and there is no way to deny their power, except through illusions we hold about ourselves. Our thoughts are never without power and if we choose to limit and destroy ourselves with them, they simply obey.

People are addicted to substances, control, safety, fear, condemnation, illness and chaos. Our addictions are really endless and all because we believe we are separate from God and each other. When we decide to allow our vision to encompass wholeness, we see a different world. I know the person I used to be and the person I have now become and they are two different people. You could say I have lived two life times in one. We all have the potential to recognize the beauty we are and to let go of everything in the way of knowing ourselves as perfect, whole, and complete.

I know for certain that if you focus on loving yourself no matter where you are at in your life, you will come to know peace. Loving yourself is really the key to the kingdom. You have to let go of all of the guilt and negative feelings you feel towards yourself and others so you can be free. The only time to make changes in your life is now. The past is gone and you can make a difference in your life and the lives of others right now. When you spend time loving yourself, you will then learn how to love others. You will extend the love you are and be extremely grateful for it. It is a freeing feeling when you know you are love and there is no need attached to it.

The most "evil" person in the world needs love. They are struggling to know themselves and have yet to discover how they are hurting themselves as well. Each of us has the potential to express deep hatred as well as experience an all-encompassing expression of love. It is the power of love that allows us the ability to make the choice each moment. There isn't a person on this earth who isn't without the choice to create their life any way they desire. There are many people who live their lives in chains because they are not aware they hold the keys to freedom.

Approval Seeking

One of the most important ingredients to spiritual awareness is learning to let go of what other people think of you. I say this because we tend to place more value on what someone else thinks rather than looking within for answers. I think it is important to let go of placing too much value on what other people think. If someone gives you a compliment or an insult they both have equal value. In other words, when you come to know yourself, opinions good or bad do not determine how you feel about yourself.

I remember a long time ago, I met a man who was a powerful instrument in healing my perceptions of the world. One of the main ideas he reinforced in my mind was to let go of what other people thought of me. Whenever we let other people's opinions determine how we feel about ourselves, we are searching outside of our own being for approval and acknowledgment.

Whenever we place value of someone else's opinion above our own, what are we doing? We are not respecting ourselves and we have not learned to listen to the inner voice which guides our thoughts and actions. Most people will feel bad about themselves when someone else speaks badly of them. Do you know that people place more faith in a negative opinion than anything else? Somehow we come to believe that negative opinions have meaning and we place great faith in them. We make them real in our minds and experience the effects of those beliefs. We have decided to believe all kinds of negative ideas about ourselves because we place faith in them.

Certainly there is a place for expert opinions concerning financial and other affairs where a person has more knowledge in a given area. However, think back to your childhood and I know you will remember at least one incident where you felt devastated by the words of another person. Why were you devastated? Because somewhere in your mind, you believed they were right. You believed they were right simply because you placed their opinion of you above your own. Learn to feel good about you, regardless of what other people say to you.

Do you know that the person isn't really seeing you anyway? They are seeing a reflection of themselves in you. They are seeing an attribute of themselves they do not like and are projecting it on to you. They have attempted to separate their mind from yours and blame you for the negative attribute. They wouldn't be able to see it in you, if it weren't present in them. Remember, there is only an illusion of separation because in reality it doesn't exist. We are one.

Why do we place such great value on someone else's negative opinion of us? If we are given a compliment, sometimes we don't even accept it. If it is negative, we come to believe it about ourselves. Why is this true for so many of us? I know we have learned to identify with the part of ourselves that needs constant approval in order to stay afloat. Of course, this is our ego, or limited self. When we learn to identify with our whole self, we also let go of the need for approval and validation. It is a very freeing feeling to know without a doubt that you are perfect, whole and complete. There is nothing that anyone can say about you that will change your real self. You may allow words to alter how you feel about your limited self but it will never change the real you.

We are a society that has learned to worship, idolize and elevate other people above ourselves. We have somehow come to believe that a person's value is determined by the way they look, act or what they do for a living. We idolize movie stars because we imagine that they are somehow better or different than ourselves. Many people in Hollywood suffer from addiction and other forms of self-destruction. Perhaps they have realized that what they thought had value, really lacked any substance at all. Is fame and fortune really all it is cracked up to be? I suppose if you thrive on the approval and validation of others, it can be extremely fulfilling. I am sure there are many reasons to strive for fame so I am not invalidating people's dreams, just their ideas of what it can do for them. People think that fame changes their value in some way and this is just not true. The bum and the star have equal rights in heaven. Each one has learned something about themselves that they didn't know before.

It is important to have a good opinion of yourself. Loving yourself is a journey worth taking. To truly love yourself involves loving your weaknesses as well as your strengths. A weakness is merely an assumption about yourself you haven't yet realized into a strength. There are no opposites in the mind of God. An attribute is a material manifestation only when perceived by the beholder as a quality they own. Where does any characteristic or quality begin? In the mind of the beholder is where any belief begins.

Freedom From Addiction

A person living with an addiction is living their life in chains. It is possible to break free from the desire to seek fulfillment outside of your own being. The substance or action you seek is only sought after because you haven't found it within yourself yet. If you are expressing complete joy in each moment, then why would you alter that feeling? What state of mind could possibly be better than the one you are in?

Simply imagine how it would feel to be free from addiction and you are half way there. If you can picture it in your mind's eye, it can be accomplished. Close your eyes, quiet your mind and bring the feeling of freedom into your being. Capture the essence of the feeling in your mind and body. Imagine a symbol that depicts this feeling of freedom for you. Whenever you feel your mind wavering into fear, focus on this symbol.

The more you focus on your strong desire to be free from the addictive behavior the greater desire you will create. Desire sets the energy in motion and is the fuel for the manifestation of anything. The intensity of your desire for an experience is what determines the possibility of its manifestation. Many people continue on with addictive behaviors without questioning a better life. They simply haven't become miserable enough to create a greater desire for freedom than bondage. If the desire to continue with the behavior is greater than the desire for freedom, the behavior continues. It is really that simple. The person experiences a perceived fulfillment from the addictive behavior that encourages its repetition. Until the person realizes there is another way to achieve peace and happiness they are likely to continue with the destructive behavior.

Make a list of the feelings you desire to have in your life without the addiction. For instance, just waking up everyday feeling good is a positive feeling you get from sobriety. There are many reasons to stay sober and your mind can agree with you rather than find reasons to drink. Your list must include things that are important to you. Remember you are searching your mind bank for reasons to stay sober.

You can also make a list of all of the reasons you are tired of the destructive behavior. Link the destructive behavior with negative qualities. Let go of what you think it can do for you because usually with an addiction the costs far outweigh the benefits. Review your list daily until it becomes easy for you to change your mind and choose freedom effortlessly. It would be a good idea to spend some time in quiet meditation following each review.

Addiction is a road that can lead you out of the hell you have created. It can lead you out of the state of mind that has caused you to believe you were trapped in the first place. It is certainly one way back to Spirit and you can turn your life around at a moment's notice. Remember, addiction is simply an instrument of healing. It is simply a tool to discovering the power of your own mind.

You must release any guilt for the wrongs you have committed in your life or it will simply perpetuate the addiction. Bless the conditions in your life, for they are an instrument of healing and not something upon which to condemn yourself. You cannot release the past by going back, living it over and feeling bad about it. You simply have to be willing to forgive yourself. I am not suggesting you continue to commit acts against yourself and others without guilt. I am saying if you want to change your life, you need to let the past go.

The whole belief system of condemnation and judgment by a God outside of us is the whole thought system that creates the negative conditions in our lives in the first place. Feeling the need to repent only places faith in the illusions we have created through fear. God doesn't feel a need to forgive us because God hasn't condemned us. We condemn and therefore feel a need to repent. Yes, we make mistakes, but as *ACIM* states, sin requires correction, not punishment. All we need to do is correct the mistakes in our lives by changing them.

Healing doesn't take place in the past. It can only take place in the present moment. I have said this before, but it is a very important point and it needs clarification. If I think I need to go back into my past and dredge up old memories in order to release them, then I have placed my faith in a time and place that no longer exists. Here and now is the only moment that exists. Our minds can certainly wander into the past, making them seem real but then we miss the moment. True healing isn't about something we do; it is about recognizing our wholeness. True health already exists; we have denied it through the illusions we hold about ourselves.

How can you know something is possible when you are suffering and freedom seems to be the farthest possibility from your mind? If one person can achieve it, then it can be done. Remember, God did not imprison your mind. You imprisoned your mind and it is up to you to free yourself. How do you free your mind? Desire it beyond anything else. Your Spirit will assist you in releasing you from the chains you have created.

Knowingness is absolute. You know something is possible when there is no doubt in your mind. If you believe it is possible to achieve freedom, then you are not quite sure yet. When you know something you do not have to put your faith into it. Do you know you have an arm or do you believe you do? I think you get the picture. Once you understand the power of knowingness then you are ready to begin. Absolute knowingness is a power that can move mountains. When you know you can be free from addiction, there is nothing that can stop you.

Addiction allowed me to understand myself. It was my road to God. There are as many roads back to our recognition of wholeness as there are people. We all know what our hurdles are in life and what it is we need to personally transcend in order to free our minds. We have an innate ability to know anything we need to know at any given moment. All we have to do is be willing to listen, by quieting our minds from the ego's voice. We always know when it is the ego speaking because the ego leads with fear. Our whole mind only speaks of love and peace.

I am writing about releasing addiction through the process of knowing ourselves because they go hand in hand. We create the problems in our lives and it is up to us to release ourselves from the constraints we have created. There is a part of us that is aware of whom we are and is readily available to teach us the way to freedom. The Holy Spirit is our guide home. In order to return home we must meet ourselves at the pearly gates. All we really need to do is be willing to release ourselves from our illusions. Our whole mind takes care of the rest.

"Unless you have a complete psychic change, you need to follow the AA way of life in order to recover from alcoholism." I remember hearing these words in some form at AA. The complete psychic change is possible and this is what I am talking about. Our mind is so powerful that we can even create lack, limitation and bondage in our lives. It is just as easy to create abundance and freedom.

Now that you have recognized it is possible to achieve freedom and you have a strong desire to change your life, then the next step involves making a commitment. In order to make a commitment, you need to firmly entrench it within your mind that you intend to reach your destination. Now you have desire, knowingness, and commitment. What more do you need to make change?

Imagine feeling fulfilled in every moment without the need for external highs. True fulfillment comes from within and is your source of joy. This is hard to understand for someone who refuses to change. The mind that wants to remain the same will not even bother to read this book. Their mind will only find reasons to continue with their behavior.

Discover the purpose your addiction serves for you. In what way does it fulfill you? What are you trying to escape from in your life? Chances are you are only trying to escape from your own thoughts. Decide which life you would like to live and focus on the one you desire. Remove your thoughts from the substance or behavior your mind is addicted to and place them where you want them to be. Rather than focusing on alcohol related thoughts, think of the feelings associated with releasing yourself from it. If you are obsessive compulsive you have to do the same. You have to retrain your mind to think differently. It doesn't matter what the addiction is; the cause is your mind and the thoughts and beliefs you hold.

The ego uses time as a reference to measure its needs. Peace and happiness are always in a future state of mind where the ego is concerned. The ego is based on addictive behaviors because salvation is always a heartbeat away. I used to think that the length of time I stayed sober was the key to maintaining sobriety. Time actually has nothing to do with it. Time only has the function you attribute to it so it has variable functions depending on which one you assign to it. In order to release yourself from your addiction, choose freedom and don't let anything get in the way of it. Go towards freedom and away from bondage. Remember, whatever you focus on becomes more prevalent in your life.

Now is the moment to change. There isn't any other moment than right now. A timeless and eternal state of being can be acknowledged here on earth. Time is really an illusion created by your mind. Place your faith in now, and fear will leave you. Now you are safe, and now you are secure. Now is where you will find peace. Envelop your mind in a sheet of knowingness because you can change.

You can accomplish years and years of sobriety without releasing yourself from the chains of addiction. People will often substitute one addiction for another and never be completely free. The person who simply stops the behavior without working on the cause is just alleviating symptoms. If you cure any illness in this manner what usually happens is the illness gets progressively worse. When one behavior is substituted for another, dysfunctional behavior is what usually occurs. I have seen it happen many times.

No matter where you are at in your life, love yourself for simply being. It will not do you any good to condemn yourself. Remember, you are simply learning about how your thoughts create and how to love yourself. Think of yourself as a little child who needs simply to accept and love him/herself. You wouldn't stand there and listen to one child berate another, so why accept berating yourself? You berate yourself all of the time and it is time to stop and take the time to send yourself love rather than fear-filled thoughts.

Releasing yourself from addiction and freeing your mind to create from love rather than fear is a process that involves dedication and persistence. It is a journey well worth taking and I encourage you to begin right now. Make a list of the freedoms you would like to discover because there is power in writing them down. It brings you clarity and you can clearly assess which direction you would like to go in life.

I suggest you do not see the ego as an enemy because then you will despise a part of yourself. The ego is not separate from you because it is your creation. However, it is a separate idea of you because God didn't create this limited version of you. When you are released from the constraints of the ego, your addictive behaviors in whatever form will also fade. Only your ego has needs that thrive on being fulfilled externally. An addictive thought can only exist in a mind that feels it is a victim of itself. "I have to change how I am feeling with a substance because I don't have the power to do it myself."

You may have to read this book over and over again until you clearly understand the principles I have discussed. I have read many books over and over until I knew the truths as a part of me. I often read something and when it feels true, I would like to know it within my being as an experience as well. I simply ask for guidance and it is received. The same is true for you of course.

At Rainbow's End is about discovering the pot of gold at the end of the rainbow. The pot of gold has nothing to do with material wealth. It is the discovering of the knowledge of your divinity and the recognition of your Spirit. It frees you from addiction by replacing your thoughts of separation with those of wholeness. No longer are you convinced you are a sinful creature who is controlled by your own mind. You have been controlling it all along by giving it the power to deceive you. Begin with the intention to be released and lie back and enjoy the ride. There is so much more to experience in life when you wake up to the truth in you.

Perhaps you have seen the movie *The Matrix*. It was an incredible movie with a spiritual basis. Even the names of the characters are biblical. If you have seen the movie and didn't catch a glimpse of the power of awakening, see it again. The story is very symbolic to me of the connection between the lives we live as awakened beings as opposed to the ones we live while dreaming. It is a powerful story about releasing the mind from the world of illusions. At least this is how I experienced it.

Examine your life from the standpoint of love verses fear. Whenever you feel yourself off center, remember you have aligned your thoughts with fear. To release yourself from fear thoughts, simply choose another one. A thought of love linked with knowingness has the power to move mountains. Love is a powerful energy and can be used for your benefit as well as your detriment. It all depends on where you choose to channel it.

Fear, ego and devil are synonymous in that you are channeling the energy of love in a negative manner. There is one force and channeling this energy into many different streams is a matter of choice. Choose your stream but be careful of which direction it will lead you.

Take note of the things you cherish most in your life. If they are things rather than people you may want to reconsider where you are channeling your energies. Treasures of the heart are everlasting and you will take them with you into eternity where you belong. Do you know that eternity is here and now? When you let go of past and future and stay in the present moment, you will discover eternity. Eternity is a state of mind that can be recognized here on earth. Just be open to letting go of judgment because this alone interferes with the connection. It is interference simply because judgment separates and once you create this split in your mind you are unable to accept union with your whole mind.

When fear encompasses your mind, step aside and view yourself from above. It is easier to release your thoughts from the emotion of fear when you imagine you are above yourself looking down upon you. It releases you from identifying with the emotions you are experiencing and makes it easier to change your thoughts. Remember that fear is chosen and you can always choose again.

Enjoy the journey. I know you will succeed in freeing your mind. You have been very successful in trapping it and the same energy can be used to free you. My thoughts and prayers are with you as you let go of the suffering and pain caused from addiction. I know how painful it is to yearn for something that causes you such immense suffering. Once you are free you will find it difficult to believe you ever desired to find happiness outside of your own being. You will never crave your addiction again.

Do you know what causes cravings? Your thoughts create them because your body isn't in charge of the show like you think. It is your mind that attributes desires and feelings to the body. Once you slow down your thoughts enough you will recognize it is the thought that comes before the experience and not the other way around. If you are having a "craving" for alcohol or anything else for that matter, change your thoughts and you will change your experience. Do you know how long it has been since I have had a craving for alcohol? I have not had a craving since I have made the connection between my mind and my body. Actually, now I am repulsed by the odor or the thought of alcohol because that is the association I have created in my mind.

If it is food you crave, then you merely need to switch the focus of the thoughts you are holding. If you continue to eat when you are not hungry, what are you feeding? You are feeding a thought of fulfillment through the pleasure of eating food. In reality you are probably not enjoying your food anyway because you are angry with yourself for eating too much. The feelings associated with overindulgence are usually guilt, condemnation and anger. You feel out of control and you want more than anything to stop eating, but you cannot because your focus is still on food. Change your thoughts and you will change your experience.

Switch your focus from food to the pleasure you would receive from having a slender, agile and healthy body. Focus on the feelings you would get from eating less and not getting so full you feel uncomfortable. All that is required of you is to change your focus. Focus on what you want rather than what you do not want. Monitor your thoughts and discover for yourself why you are over eating. Make two lists and include your feelings associated with food. On one side put the feelings you would like to have and on the other side put down the ones you do not like to experience. Any time you have a thought that brings the negative feelings with it, change it to the one that brings positive results. If you overeat, you feel full and uncomfortable. Rather than focusing on the feelings of heaviness and fatigue associated with overeating; focus on lightness and energy associated with eating less.

I have heard people say that really fat people do not feel full because their body doesn't give them the full signal. They don't feel satisfied because their body doesn't produce a certain chemical in the brain. Their body doesn't produce it because their mind hasn't told it too. Your mind gives the instructions to your body and not the other way around. No, I am not a doctor so you can choose whether or not to heed my advice. But I will ask you, has a doctor been able to help you lose weight? Has a doctor been able to help you change your mind about what you would like to experience in your life? If so, that is wonderful. I do not believe doctors are the only people that are qualified to give advice.

I only have a bachelor's degree but life is a school when we are willing to learn. I have chosen to live and learn from my life. I have learned to transcend addiction and experience says a lot. You have a choice to recognize whether or not what I am telling you are truths. If your life is working for you, then so be it.

I am simply suggesting another way to look at your life. If you are not the creator of your experiences, then who is? I used to think that alcoholism was something I brought with me into this life. I was destined to be an alcoholic for life. I know now that it was simply a result of the beliefs I held about my life and the thoughts that resulted from them. I have been cured of alcoholism because I have changed my mind. You can do the same no matter what your addiction may be. The cause of addiction is the same. You are not a victim of your body. Rather, you have chosen to be a victim of your own mind.

So let's say you have begun the road to the recovery of your own personal power. There may be times when your feelings waiver because you are so accustomed to allowing other people to govern your experience. Many times, your mind may confront you and tell you that you are being ridiculous. Do not let this stop you. Let it be a reminder of the control your lesser self seeks to exert over you.

Perhaps you have a renewed sense of adventure. You can use this as fuel to continue on with your mission of rediscovering yourself. You can always find reasons to go forward and seek the peace you desire. Just remember, you are exactly what you are thinking about at this moment. You can easily choose again if you do not like the experience you are having right now. Now is the only moment there is so if you want to change the way you are viewing your life, then now is the time.

The moon appears to be more full at times than others. Of course this is only an illusion because the moon remains the same. Everyone knows this, however at times they allow their eyes to convince them otherwise. Sometimes we see the world the way it appears to be rather than the way it really is. Our eyes can deceive us because the world is full of illusions and truth cannot always be seen with the naked eye.

So be open to truth and acknowledge it in whatever form it appears. I can assure you that your eyes can deceive you. Your Spirit will guide you. You rely heavily upon your five senses in this world but they can also be misleading. You are equipped with an inner knowingness or intuitive sense that will let you know whatever you need to know in the moment. Oftentimes this inner sense is discounted and after time we drown out the sense all together. Fear then comes into play because we find ourselves trapped by the reliability of senses that are inadequate. Feelings of safety and security are lost because they are based on receiving information from external cues. Our inner knowingness is a part of who we are and it has all the information available that it needs at any given moment. Even time and space do not limit this sense. Simply be open to reconnecting with your inner knowingness. You always know when you denied your inner voice because of your experience. Do not condemn yourself for it; just acknowledge it so that next time you will be more prepared to listen.

Surrender and Release

What does it mean to surrender and release? I am sure you have had more than one experience that has shown you the power behind the idea of relinquishing control. When you let go of the need to control a situation, you also let go of the energy in place that is counterproductive to the state you want to achieve. How many times have you heard of a couple that want to get pregnant very badly and can't, so they adopt. Shortly afterwards, they become pregnant. There is power behind letting go because there is not a resistive force to stop the flow of energy in accomplishing your dream.

It is important to surrender and release everything in our life so that the natural order of life flows without interruption. When we try to control everything in our life with certain expectations or plans, then we are using fear to lay the course of our life. We can know a dream we wish to achieve, but then we have to let it go and act only when we are guided to act. We do not have to dispel a lot of wasteful energy by acting on impulse. We can center ourselves and wait for the appropriate guidance to act. We will always know what to do to accomplish our goal in the most efficient manner.

Remember, our whole self knows everything we need to know including the best way to live our life. If we remain in the present moment and allow the Holy Spirit to guide our life, then our life will flow easily and effortlessly. We create resistance when we feel a need to control the outcome. We obviously have doubt in our minds when we fearfully create images in our minds of how things need to be. In order to surrender and release we have to let go of how we think things ought to be.

For example, the company my husband is working for right now is on the brink of closing down. I need to have faith that if one door closes another door will open. If I spend my time needlessly fearing bankruptcy or the worst possible outcome, then what am I doing? I am placing my faith in a fearful outcome. I have surrendered and released the situation by knowing that if change occurs I don't have to be fearful of it. Change is frightening for many people because they don't know the outcome. They think they somehow know how their life is going to be whenever things remain the same. This is an illusion because change is always just around the corner. Life would be so boring without it.

It is a tremendously freeing feeling to surrender and release your mind from controlling everything in your life. What a burden it is to hang on to all the needless clutter and garbage you pick up along the way of your journey. Today is the only day we need concern ourselves with. Right now is the only moment there is and to place your faith in fear is to place your faith in the past or future. In reality you are placing your faith in an illusive moment because past and future are never really here. Does tomorrow ever really come? Can you ever really go back into your past?

One of the most important steps we can take in life is surrender and release. Try it for a moment and see how it feels. Give all your thoughts and worries to your whole self. Your whole self knows exactly what to do in any given moment because your whole mind sees the bigger picture. Your limited self only sees what is right in front of you.

It is a rather freeing feeling to know without a doubt you are cared for and protected. You may only experience this feeling for moments at a time but nevertheless it is reassuring.

We can spend so much of our time in worry and fear. Surrender and release is a choice we can make effortlessly when we realize the benefits. Life flows effortlessly when there are no damns in the way. The only impediments to anything in life are our thoughts and beliefs. When we learn to let go and let God, we open the force and make room for the creation of miracles in our lives. For a moment, visualize complete release from fear. It is fear that creates the boundaries and limitations we experience.

Surrender and release your worries and fears to your whole self. Remember there is nothing your mind cannot do as long as it has your cooperation. Imagine climbing a mountain and every moment you have a fear thought, you take a step back down. How long would it take you to get to the top? If you have a lot of fearful thoughts you may never reach it.

Whenever I have fearful thoughts in relation to my writing, I have a difficult time making any progress. I had given a copy of my writing to my father to proof read for me. I noticed quickly how easily my mind drifted to doubt and fear. My father would not have judged my book negatively so my fears were not about him. It was about the fears in my own mind. I know not everyone is going to enjoy reading my book and I also know that is okay. There will be just as many who benefit from it. I experienced how easily it was to create doubt because it is just a thought away. I decided to take back the copy of my manuscript until I was completely finished. I did not want to have anything interfere with its completion.

I had asked the angels for guidance at a moment when I was experiencing self-doubt. I asked for a sign and I was pretty specific about the sign. I said, "Angels, please show me a rainbow in a manner in which I would least expect to see it." We went off to my son's playground at school where he was having a play day. It was nearing the end of the school year and they were having a picnic at the playground. Soon after we got there a little girl came up to me and pointed at her cheek. She said, "Look," as she pointed at the rainbow on her face.

Last night a rainbow appeared above our home. It wasn't raining or anything. It was partly cloudy and I have never seen anything quite like it. The rainbow was upside down as if it were smiling. I have to wonder if that wasn't some reinforcement as well. Nevertheless, I received an answer. For some reason I questioned whether or not I should be writing this book at all. I know now I can let the doubts go. After all what really matters is that I love writing. I also want to share my experiences with the world because it may help someone else.

If you don't like what you're thinking, then change your mind. It is that simple and we tend to complicate our lives with doubts and fears. Surrendering and releasing control involves letting go of these thoughts and replacing them with knowingness and trust. It is always a choice between fear and trust. Why do we think it is easier to be fearful? Perhaps it is because we are so accustomed to responding in this manner. We can change habits and that is really all it is. We have learned to respond to events with fear through repetition.

It has been approximately three months since we heard the supposed fate of my husband's job. I had decided to let go and let God and pray for the company's survival. The last information I heard from my husband was that the company is doing incredibly well. When we let go and let God, we can expect the miracle.

We can learn to live in a state of knowingness and peace. Let's see, we can choose to trust in a positive outcome to any event or we can choose fear. Fear puts our mind in a state of panic and then we cannot see any other options. We block out our experience of peace the moment we choose fear. Why is fear so appealing? What does it have to offer that peace doesn't? I can tell you one thing; I choose peace right here and now. If you can think of a good reason to hold on to fear then let me know.

Conclusion

What greater purpose can life serve then the recognition of our divinity? The ego has many ideas of what a purpose is in life. The purpose that serves the ego is one of glorification and separation. The purpose of the Spirit is discovering the love we are and sharing this love with the world. The glory comes directly from the experience of this knowledge and not from the world.

We would like to think that we all have a separate purpose that is special. The ego likes to think in terms of being special because that is its identification. We strive to be better than others and this is not possible. We are equal in the mind of God. Whenever we are thinking competitively, we are thinking from an ego state. Sure enough, in this world we have different levels of income and social status. Nevertheless, we are all equal in Spirit. We are one.

Whenever you contemplate thoughts of creation, you superimpose these thoughts onto the canvas of life. For an instant, let's assume you have been wrong about your identity as a child of God. Through the power of your own creative potential you created a separate being, other than what was originally intended for you. Let's say God created you in his/her image. Do you really think God would create anything less than perfect love?

Whatever ideas you hold about yourself are the ideas you live by. Your world is a direct reflection of whatever ideas and beliefs you hold about you. God created you perfect but you have chosen to see yourself as separate and alone. You have been mistaken and you simply need to open your mind to experiencing yourself the way God intended for you. You have placed limitations on your experience, not

God. God is not to blame for the world the ego has enslaved. God is not responsible for fear because it is not a part of God's mind.

Your purpose in life is to know yourself as God knows you. Jesus, like many other masters, is a channel for the perfect love of God. Jesus doesn't want to be worshipped. He wants you to live life in a manner consistent with who you really are as a child of God. When you let go of fear and separation, you will be free to express the love of God in your life.

Your purpose in life is not to strive for greatness for you already are greater than you can imagine. You simply need to recognize the greatness comes from the power of God. Whenever we separate ourselves from each other, we need glory and recognition. There is no greater glory than reuniting with the love of God. God didn't create hardships, disease, or death, the ego did. I know this is true because God is love and it just would not make sense otherwise. Just be willing to stretch your mind and open up to the rewards of the world God created for you to experience.

Limitation is a word created from an ego state. Life and death are interchangeable, meaning the only difference is in the mind that cherishes one state of existence for another. Death is often viewed as the key to freedom. The only way to be free from your limited self is to see yourself as free. You can be free here and now. Eternity is in the present moment. It is not something to be feared after death. People fear going to hell for an eternity. That is ridiculous. God is not punitive, but the ego most certainly is destructive and in more than one way.

I cannot understand how people can fear God. I suppose they believe the love of God demands sacrifice and this is so far from truth. As a young child, when I learned the story of Jesus dying on the cross, I couldn't make the connection either. How could one person's detriment have anything to do with another's well-being? Sacrifice is absolutely an ego term that simply creates fear. Jesus was merely teaching us the ability to transcend the body and the resurrection is where the focus ought to be placed. Jesus is very much alive because the body is not real. Of course he has the power to experience a body at will. There are many other masters of consciousness and you too have the power to renew your connection to the divine mind.

A few years ago I was shown how the power of God could even keep you warm. I was running one morning and my hands were freezing. I hadn't realized how cold it was outside and so I was unprepared. I had the thought that maybe I should focus on my hands getting warmer. Immediately I felt a surge of warmth through my hands and body. I found it really amazing. The next morning I went running without any gloves. I practically froze to death I was so cold. Apparently I had more faith in the cold this time and the same method didn't work for me. I think maybe God was just showing me the power of faith. *"In this world, you believe you are sustained by everything but God. Your faith is placed in the most trivial and insane symbols; pills, money, "protective" clothing, influence, prestige, being liked, knowing the right people, and an endless list of forms of nothingness that you endow with magical powers. (ACIM, II. p.79, 1;2,3) "All these things are your replacements for the Love of God. All these things are cherished to ensure a body identification. They are songs of praise to the ego. Do not put your faith in the worthless. It will not sustain you."(ACIM, II. p.79, 2; 1-5)*

It is the love and power of God that really sustains us. We attribute this power to so many different external sources and it is simply not truth. When you awaken to the truth you will be free from the constraints and dictates of society. The world as you see it now is the way it is because you have allowed society to dictate to you the way it is. There is no one reality. Remember this and do not agree with anyone about the way anything is because nothing is written in stone except the laws of God. ACIM says there are no laws but God's. I have to agree with it simply because it makes perfect sense. The laws the world created do not make sense. *"You really think you would starve unless you have stacks of green paper strips and piles of metal discs. You really think a small round pellet or some fluid pushed into your veins through a sharpened needle will ward off disease and death. You really think you are alone unless another body is with you."(ACIM, II. p.134, 3; 2-4) "It is insanity that thinks these things. You call them laws, and put them under different names in a long catalogue of rituals that have no use and serve no purpose. You think you must obey the "laws" of medicine, of economics and of health. Protect the body, and you will be saved." (ACIM, II. p.134,4;1-4)* We have convinced our own minds we must follow by the laws of the world. Expand your own mind and allow the Holy Spirit to show you another way of life.

The world focuses on the body as the means for salvation. Many people are even afraid to be alone. People have a tendency to feel sorry for someone because they live "all alone". We are never alone. Feelings of separateness and isolation are created from the mind that thinks it is real. We are not separate and we are always connected to source.

The other day my parents took the children for a couple of days. My husband works all day and all of a sudden I had all of this time to myself. I haven't had time like this to myself for a while so I absolutely cherished it. At first I had thoughts of fear and I recognized them immediately so I let them go. Why do we tend to fear being alone? What are we afraid of?

I have never been at this place of peace in my life and so this was the first time I had time with myself without fear. I didn't have to busy myself or feel a need to drown out my feelings with a substance. All I had to do was make the connection in my mind between the thoughts and the feelings I wanted to experience. I used to fear being alone and now I know why. I thought that if I were alone I would have to experience certain feelings that I would rather avoid. The truth is, I am never alone and how I feel is up to me.

For the first time in my life, I really enjoyed being with me. I have learned to love who I am. The person I didn't love was just a belief connected with fear. It was an idea with negative effects. I sent negative messages to myself and experienced the effects of those thoughts. It actually had nothing to do with who I really am. Now I enjoy being with me and I realize there is nothing to fear about it at all. After all, some people feel lonely in a crowd, so it has absolutely nothing to do with other people. Remember, peace and freedom cannot be found outside of ourselves, so if we are looking there we need to place the focus back where it belongs.

Freedom can be achieved when our wholeness is recognized. There isn't anything that isn't possible when we let go of the illusions we hold about ourselves. I read another sign in front of a church yesterday that blew my mind. It said that freedom came at the price of great sacrifice. There is no sacrifice in freedom and recognizing our Spirit. It is the most wonderful experience there is and it would greatly benefit us if we let go of the belief in sacrifice.

Jesus intended to free our minds from the belief in sacrifice. Jesus was and continues to be a powerful man. The crucifixion never would have occurred if Jesus didn't allow it to. He was not a victim in any way. He chose it to prove a point. Death can be overcome and the body is not real. At the time of his life, sacrifice was placed at a great value. He wanted to stop the value of sacrifice in man's mind through the ultimate sacrifice. Nevertheless, it continues.

You will not come to know yourself as long as you feel sacrifice is necessary. You will avoid it like the plague. Who in the world would do something that came at a great price? The rewards of the kingdom are truly remarkable and I can assure you, they are not at a great cost. It is the ego's thought system that is linked with sacrifice. If your thoughts or beliefs include fear in any manner, know with a certainty it is not about God. The thoughts God would have you think are fearless.

If there is any sacrifice to be made it would include the value of the body in relation to the mind. The world places value on the body above the mind rather than seeing it as an extension of the mind. When we give up identifying ourselves as a body we will no longer feel sacrifice is necessary. It isn't a sacrifice to give up something that doesn't hold any value in our minds. When we succumb to the knowledge of who we are, all of the idols we worshipped needlessly attempting to achieve a sense of importance and value, fall away. They fall away because they are no longer needed. There is nothing we can achieve in this world that will equal the value we are given through the power of God. God created our value when we were created. Any attempt at creating our own self-worth is ego-directed because we do not need to strive for something we already are.

We were created perfect, whole and complete. Anything less than this is simply a creation of the ego. God did not create imperfection, we did. We created it when we began to see ourselves as separate from God. We began to worship him instead of viewing ourselves as equals. Many people also treat their children the way we expect God to treat us. We somehow believe we are superior simply because they are in little bodies. Their Spirits were created at the same moment that ours were created.

It is important to note that when we become willing to give up this identification, we begin to see the love we are, reflected in everyone we meet. We no longer feel a need to ridicule or attack others because we see everyone as a part of ourselves. We acknowledge the attack from within rather from out there. We no longer can justify attack in any form for it disturbs our own peace. We now know with a certainty that anything we think, we feel and we guard our thoughts carefully.

Suppose for a moment someone attacks you with anger regarding an experience the person is projecting onto you. You feel it is an unfair attack for the situation has obviously been created in their mind. How do you respond to this person's attack? Do you reciprocate the attack because you feel it is unjust, or do you let it slide by you knowing it is illusive anyway? All attack is illusive no matter how fair or unfair the attack may seem to be. It is illusive because it is guided by the ego. Any time you respond with fear and anger you are allowing your actions to be dictated by the ego.

When you recognize everyone as a part of you, you can decide not to use anger or attack thoughts. What do they accomplish except the creation of more anger and fear? We can refuse to identify with these feelings and share feelings of unconditional acceptance with everyone we meet. When we identify ourselves as our Spirit rather than the body we seem to inhabit, we feel connected to all of life. We are responsible for every thought and feeling we extend, for they become a part of us as well.

We cannot be rid of attack thoughts by focusing our attention on letting them go. What happens is we get what we focus upon. Rather than focusing on the feelings you want to let go of, focus on the feelings you want to experience. We often condemn ourselves for anger and fear and this only perpetuates the problem. Remember, wherever we place our attention is where we will be. Whenever you find yourself getting angry, stop, take a deep breath and ask for a spiritual rather than an ego-driven perspective. You will soon recognize that peace is the only choice that makes any sense.

When we discover our Spirit, the problems in our life slip away. They are only there because we have allowed the ego to create the world of illusions where they exist. Addiction itself is an illusion the ego upholds to ensure its survival. Seeking outside of ourselves for peace and happiness is what creates the prison in our own minds. We become trapped by our relentless search for feelings of peace and happiness in all of the wrong places. When you are tired of the life you have been living you may be willing to discover another way to live. It all begins with intention and desire. The key to learning anything new involves first knowing that you do not know. Empty your mind of everything you know to be true and be willing to let your Spirit reveal truth to you. You have to make room for truth. Do you find it difficult to teach someone who is sure they have all of the answers?

Addictions will fall away as a natural expression of your Spirit. Your mind will change and you will not think the same way anymore. When you feel complete, there isn't a constant striving to attain it. You are not looking for fulfillment, when you already are fulfilled. Seek to know thyself and quiet your mind enough to listen to God. You have to dissect your mind and let go of everything you no longer need. It is a process of elimination. You learn to let go of everything that is not a part of the real you.

Let's assume you have been living your life from the standpoint of physical reality rather than a spiritual focus. Sure enough whenever you have needed help or assistance it was time to rely on the spiritual side, but it was only for emergencies. Face it; most of us live our lives securing all of our needs from external sources rather than from within. Our lives are too busy to take the time to really come to know ourselves. Maybe you attend church weekly and you think you are feeding your Spiritual side but you go home and continue to live your life from the standpoint of fear.

God is found within the silence of your own mind. If you don't take the time to be in the silence, you will not learn to listen to the guidance that will direct your life easily and effortlessly. Your life can be so much easier when you learn to tune in to the divine guidance that is always available to you. I am writing the very words in this book through the process of listening to my Spirit. At times I can hear whole sentences at a time. I have learned to listen through the processes I am writing about now. Every night before I go to bed, I take the time to meditate and connect with my Spirit. Some nights I experience moments of silence and other times I receive valuable information. You will be amazed at what you can learn directly from your own Spirit.

There are many people that spend their lifetime learning from what other people tell them is truth rather than going within and listening to their own guidance. The problem with listening solely to other people is that we can often be misled. Seeking outside of ourselves for all of the answers prohibits you from listening to your own feelings. You may believe what someone tells you but fail to listen to your own feelings about it. If you deny your own Spirit the chance to teach you, then you are encouraging the egos survival.

Sure enough you can learn from other people. God speaks through everyone. It is the denial of listening to your own guidance that leads to problems. When you know who you are and listen to your own guidance you can avoid so many catastrophes in life. The guidance is available to you even with the little things in life.

I know of people that are the exact same person they were twenty years ago because they have never asked the question, who am I? They continue to live their lives based upon the ideas they have about themselves even if they are dysfunctional. They do not change their behavior because they believe it defines them rather than the other way around. They are helpless to change because it is just the way they are. If we never ask and take the time to listen, how are we supposed to learn anything real?

Groups and organizations can keep people from challenging their existing beliefs. It can be particularly difficult for someone to break free from them. The group pressure often forces people to conform regardless of their feelings. Many people have a need to belong and they fulfill this need by agreeing with other people simply for the fulfillment of their perceived needs. People that do not conform to the group do not belong in them for long and so there is a fear to conform.

Some religions encourage fear and separation through the use of prohibitions. Certain clothes are prohibited or anything that encourages the belief in shame and sin. People are taught to feel bad about whom they are and people willingly conform to such destructive beliefs. God would never teach you such destructive ideas about who you are. God is about love and so many beliefs about God stem from fear. That is the only shame here. People fear the body in so many ways. After all it is the ego's creation. Nevertheless, God would not teach you the way out of fear, through the use of fear.

It is time to wake up to the truth. Of course there are many people that will spend many more lifetimes dreaming because they will not think for themselves. People want to be liked and they worship approval because they think it matters. What really matters is we learn to love and respect ourselves from within rather than allowing others to define us. We cannot please everyone but we can learn to please ourselves. Take the time to be with you. It is the greatest accomplishment in life to know you. Everything else is simply a diversion.

I asked for a sign when *At Rainbow's End* was near completion. I didn't want to stop writing before it was complete. I also knew I had to alleviate some fears regarding its release. This morning I had a vision of a game board. At the end was a square with writing on it. The feelings came along with the words so I knew it was my sign. I

AT RAINBOW'S END

could read it clearly and it said, "Strength; Rainbow's ending."

There is a way home to the real you. You have been on your way ever since you left. Unfortunately you keep taking the scenic view and you have been misled down many roads. Because of this you have become lost. You can find your way home once again. You will need maps to assist you but they are all around you. You simply need to ask. Remember to ask; always ask.

"HAWK SHE SOARS"

An autumn day, wind in my hair, the sky was gray
Riding along I whispered with doubt and fear
I needed something to appear

So many questions what if things don't work out
Is now the right time?
Please give me a sign

Like magic she appeared on the right side of the road
She left her perch taking with her my heavy load
She flew beside me so close I could almost touch her
Then she flew higher and higher
My soul went right along beside her

Chorus:
Hawk she soars, higher and higher
With grace and beauty
No fear to falter her, nothing could alter her
Powerful peaceful flight
Hawk she soars

I have found my freedom keeping both feet on the ground
The chains I have made are broken and no longer hold me down.
I too can soar each day
She showed me the way

She taught me how to look at the world with new insight
Where nothing seems too big or impossible
My soul has no boundaries
Nothing to hold me down
Now I have faith in my own flight

Chorus:
I can soar, higher and higher
With grace and beauty
No fear to falter me
Nothing can alter my powerful, peaceful flight
I can soar, Hawk she soars, in my soul

By Julie Dregne

Reference

References are cited for the second edition of A COURSE IN MIRACLES, February 1993. The references are in brackets abbreviated as ACIM followed by Text I or II, then page number, paragraph and sentence. Section I of A COURSE IN MIRACLES is Text, section II is the WORKBOOK FOR STUDENTS. Section three is the MANUAL FOR TEACHERS.

A COURSE IN MIRACLES was published by the
FOUNDATION FOR INNER PEACE
P.O. Box 598
Mill Valley, CA 94942

Portions of *A Course in Miracles*® copyright 1975, 1992, 1996 reprinted by permission of the *Foundation for A Course in Miracles, Inc.*® (www.facim.org). All rights reserved.

A Course in Miracles® is a registered trademark of the *Foundation for A COURSE IN MIRACLES*®

The ideas represented herein are the personal interpretation and understanding of the author and are not necessarily endorsed by the copyright holder of A Course in Miracles®.